$p.18$
$p.71$
$p.168$
228

WOODROW WILSON AND THE WORLD WAR

TEXTBOOK EDITION

∴

THE CHRONICLES
OF AMERICA SERIES
ALLEN JOHNSON
EDITOR

GERHARD R. LOMER
CHARLES W. JEFFERYS
ASSISTANT EDITORS

SIGNING THE PEACE TREATY, JUNE 28, 1919
From the unfinished painting by John C. Johansen, N.A.

Courtesy of the National Art Committee

WOODROW WILSON AND THE WORLD WAR

A CHRONICLE OF OUR OWN TIMES

BY CHARLES SEYMOUR

NEW HAVEN: YALE UNIVERSITY PRESS
TORONTO: GLASGOW, BROOK & CO.
LONDON: HUMPHREY MILFORD
OXFORD UNIVERSITY PRESS

CONTENTS

CONTENTS

ILLUSTRATION

WOODROW WILSON AND THE WORLD WAR

CHAPTER I

WILSON THE EXECUTIVE

WHEN, on March 4, 1913, Woodrow Wilson entered the White House, the first Democratic president elected in twenty years, no one could have guessed the importance of the rôle which he was destined to play. While business men and industrial leaders bewailed the mischance that had brought into power a man whose attitude towards vested interests was reputed none too friendly, they looked upon him as a temporary inconvenience. Nor did the increasingly large body of independent voters, disgusted by the "stand-pattism" of the Republican machine, regard Wilson much more seriously; rather did they place their confidence in a reinvigoration of the Grand Old Party through the

1

progressive leadership of Roosevelt, whose enthusiasm and practical vision had attracted the approval of more than four million voters in the preceding election, despite his lack of an adequate political organization. Even those who supported Wilson most whole-heartedly believed that his work would lie entirely within the field of domestic reform; little did they imagine that he would play a part in world affairs larger than had fallen to any citizen of the United States since the birth of the country.

The new President was fifty-six years old. His background was primarily academic, a fact which, together with his Scotch-Irish ancestry, the Presbyterian tradition of his family, and his early years spent in the South, explains much in his character at the time when he entered upon the general political stage. After graduating from Princeton in 1879, where his career gave little indication of extraordinary promise, he studied law, and for a time his shingle hung out in Atlanta. He seemed unfitted by nature, however, for either pleasure or success in the practice of the law. Reserved and cold, except with his intimates, he was incapable of attracting clients in a profession and locality where ability to "mix" was a prime qualification. A certain lack of tolerance for the failings of his fellow mortals may have combined with his Presbyterian conscience to disgust him with the hard give-and-take of the struggling lawyer's life. He sought escape in graduate work in history and politics at Johns Hopkins, where, in 1886, he received his Ph.D. for a thesis entitled *Congressional Government*, a study remarkable for clear thinking and felicitous expression. These qualities characterized his work as a professor at Bryn Mawr and Wesleyan and paved his path to an appointment on the Princeton faculty in 1890, as Professor of Jurisprudence and Politics.

Despite his early distaste to the career of practicing lawyer, Wilson was by no means the man to bury himself in academic research. He lacked the scrupulous patience and the willingness to submerge his own personality which are characteristic of the scientific scholar. His gift was for generalization, and his writings were marked by clarity of thought and wealth of phrase, rather than by profundity. But such qualities brought him remarkable success as a lecturer and essayist, and constant practice gave him a fluency, a vocal control, and a power of verbal expression which assured distinction at the frequent public meetings and dinners where he was called upon to speak. Professional interest in the science of government furnished him with topics of far wider import than the ordinary pedagogue cares to handle, and he became, even as professor, well known outside of Princeton. His influence, already broad in the educational and not without some recognition in the political world, was extended in 1902, when he was chosen President of the University.

During the succeeding eight years Wilson enjoyed his first taste of executive power, and certain traits which he then displayed deserve brief notice. Although a "conservative" in his advocacy of the maintenance of the old-time curriculum, based upon the ancient languages and mathematics, and in his opposition to the free elective system, he proved an inflexible reformer as regards methods of instruction, the efficiency of which he was determined to establish. He showed a ruthless resolution to eliminate what he looked upon as undemocratic social habits among the undergraduates, and did not hesitate to cut loose from tradition, regardless of the prejudice thereby aroused against him. As an executive he evoked intense admiration and virulent dislike; the Board of Trustees and the alumni body were alike divided between enthusiastic support and bitter anathematization of the measures he proposed. What seems obvious is that many graduates sympathized with his purposes but were alienated by his methods. His strength lay chiefly in the force of his appeal to democratic sentiment; his weakness in complete inability to conciliate opponents.

At the moment when the issue of the struggle at Princeton was still undecided, opportunity was given Wilson to enter political life; an ambition for such a career had evidently stirred him in early days and was doubtless resuscitated by his success as a public speaker. While President of Princeton he had frequently touched upon public issues, and so early as 1906 Colonel George Harvey had mentioned him as a possible President of the United States. From that time he was often considered as available for political office, and in 1910, with New Jersey stirred by a strong popular movement against boss-rule, he was tendered the nomination for Governor of that State. He accepted and proved an ideal candidate. Though supported by the Democratic machine, which planned to elect a reformer and then control him, Wilson won the adherence of independents and progressive Republicans by his promise to break the power of the boss system, and by the clarity of his plans for reform.

His appeals to the spirit of democracy and morality, while they voiced nothing new in an electoral campaign, rang with unusual strength and sincerity. The State, which had gone Republican by eighty-two thousand two years before, now elected Wilson its Governor by a plurality of forty-nine thousand.

He retained office in New Jersey for only two years. During that period he achieved a high degree of success. Had he served longer it is impossible to say what might have been his ultimate position, for as at Princeton, elements of opposition had begun to coalesce against him and he had found no means to disarm them. As Governor, he at once declared himself head of the party and by a display of firm activity dominated the machine. The Democratic boss, Senator James Smith, was sternly enjoined from seeking reëlection to the Senate, and when, in defiance of promises and the wish of the voters as expressed at the primaries, he attempted to run, Wilson entered the lists and so influenced public opinion and the Legislature that the head of the machine received only four votes. Attempts of the Democratic machine to combine with the Republicans, in order to nullify the reforms which Wilson had promised in his campaign, proved equally futile. With strong popular support, constantly ex ercising his influence both in party conferences and on the Legislature, the Governor was able to trans late into law the most important of the measures demanded by the progressives. He himself summed up the essence of the situation when he said: "The moment the forces in New Jersey that had resisted reform realized that the people were backing new men who meant what they had said, they realized that they dare not resist them. It was not the per sonal force of the new officials; it was the moral strength of their backing that accomplished the extraordinary result." Supreme confidence in the force of public opinion exerted by the common man characterizes much of Wilson's political philosophy, and the position in the world which he was to enjoy for some months towards the end of the war rested upon the same basis.

In 1912 came the presidential election. The split in the Republican forces promised if it did not absolutely guarantee the election of a Democrat, and when the party convention met at Baltimore in June, excitement was more than ordinarily in tense. The conservative elements in the party were divided. The radicals looked to Bryan for leader ship, although his nomination seemed out of the question. Wilson had stamped himself as an anti-machine progressive, and if the machine conservatives threatened he might hope for support from the Nebraskan orator. From the first the real contest appeared to be between Wilson and Champ Clark, who although hardly a conservative, was backed for the moment by the machine leaders. The deciding power was in Bryan's hand, and as the strife between conservatives and radicals waxed hot, he turned to the support of Wilson. On the forty-sixth ballot Wilson was nominated. With division in the Republican ranks, with his record in New Jersey for legislative accomplishment, and winning many independent votes through a succession of effective campaign speeches, Wilson more than fulfilled the highest of Democratic hopes. He received on election day only a minority of all the votes cast, but his majority in the electoral college was overwhelming.

The personality of an American President has seldom undergone so much analysis with such unsatisfactory results; almost every discussion of Wilson's characteristics leads to the generation of heat rather than light. Indeed the historian of the future may ask whether it is as important, in this age of democracy, to know exactly what sort of man he was as to know what the people thought he was. And yet in the case of a statesman who was to play a rôle of supreme importance in the affairs of the country and the world, it is perhaps more than a matter of merely personal interest to underline his salient traits. Let it be premised that a logical and satisfactory analysis is well-nigh impossible, for his nature is self-contradictory, subject to gusts of temperament, and he himself has pictured the struggle that has gone on between the impulsive Irish and the cautious Scotch elements in him. Thus it is that he has handled similar problems in different ways at different times, and has produced upon different persons diametrically opposed impressions.

As an executive, perhaps his most notable characteristic is the will to dominate. This does not mean that he is the egocentric autocrat pictured by his opponents, for in conference he is apt to be tolerant of the opinions of others, by no means dictatorial in manner, and apparently anxious to obtain facts on both sides of the argument. An unfriendly critic, Mr. E. J. Dillon, has said of him at Paris that "he was a very good listener, an intelligent questioner, and amenable to argument whenever he felt free to give practical effect to his conclusions." Similar evidence has been offered by members of his Cabinet. But unquestionably, in reaching a conclusion he resents pressure and he permits no one to make up his mind for him; he is, said the German Ambassador, "a recluse and lonely worker." One of his enthusiastic admirers has written: "Once in possession of every fact in the case, the President withdraws, commences the business of consideration, comparison, and assessment, and then emerges with a decision." From such a decision it is difficult to shake him and continued opposition serves merely to stiffen his resolution. Wherever the responsibility is his, he insists upon the finality of his judgment. Those who have worked with him have remarked upon his eagerness, once he has decided a course of action, to carry it into practical effect. The President of the Czecho-Slovak Republic, Thomas G. Masaryk, said that of all the men he had met, "your visionary, idealistic President is by far and away the most intensely practical." One of the Big Four at Paris remarked: "Wilson works. The rest of us play, comparatively speaking. We Europeans can't keep up with a man who travels a straight path with such a swift stride, never looking to right or left." But with all his eagerness for practical effect he is notably less efficient in the execution than in the formation of policies.

Wilson lacks, furthermore, the power of quick decision which is apt to characterize the masterful executive. He is slow to make up his mind, a trait that results partly, perhaps, from his Scotch blood and partly from his academic training. Except for his steadfast adherence to what he regards as basic principles, he might rightly be termed an opportunist. For he is prone to temporize, anxious to prevent an issue from approaching a crisis, evidently in the hope that something may "turn up" to improve the situation and obviate the necessity of conflict. "Watchful waiting" in the Mexican crises and his attitude towards the belligerents during the first two years of the European war are cases in point. There are instances of impulsive action on his part, when he has not waited for advice or troubled to acquire exact knowledge of the facts underlying a situation, but such occasions have been infrequent.

Wilson's dislike of advice has been widely advertized. It is probably closer to the truth to say that he is naturally suspicious of advisers unless he is certain that their basic point of view is the same as his own. This is quite different from saying that he wants only opinions that coincide with his own and that he immediately dispenses with advisers who disagree with him. Colonel House, for example, who for five years exerted constant influence on his policy, frequently advanced opinions quite at variance from those of the President, but such differences did not weaken House's influence inasmuch as Wilson felt that they were both starting from the same angle towards the same point. Prejudiced though he seemed to be against "financiers," Wilson took the opinions of Thomas W. Lamont at Paris, because the underlying object of both, the acquisition of a secure peace, was identical. It is true, however, that with the exception of Colonel House, Wilson's advisers have been in the main purveyors of facts rather than colleagues in the formation of policies. Wilson has generally been anxious to receive facts which might help him to build his policy, as will be attested by those who worked with him at Paris.[1] But he was less inter-

[1] Mr. Lamont says of the President at Paris: "I never saw a man more ready and anxious to consult than he. . . . President Wilson did not have a well-organized secretarial staff. He did far too much of the work himself, studying until late at night papers and documents that he should have largely delegated to some discreet aides. He was by all odds, the hardest worked man at the Conference; but the failure to delegate more of his work was not due

ested in the opinions of his advisers, especially when it came to principles and not details, for he decides principles for himself. In this sense his Cabinet was composed of subordinates rather than counselors. Such an attitude is, of course, characteristic of most modern executives and has been intensified by war conditions. The summary disregard of Lansing, shown by Wilson at Paris, was less striking than the snubbing of Balfour by Lloyd George, or the cold brutality with which Clemenceau treated the other French delegates.

General conviction of Wilson's autocratic nature has been intensified by his choice of assistants, who have not as a rule enjoyed public confidence. He debarred himself from success in the matter of appointments, in the first place, by limiting his range of choice through unwillingness to have about him those who did not share his point of view. It is more epigrammatic than exact to say that he was the sole unit in the Government giving

---

to any inherent distrust that he had of men — and certainly not to any desire to 'run the whole show' himself — but simply to the lack of facility in knowing how to delegate work on a large scale. In execution we all have a blind spot in some part of our eye. President Wilson's was in his inability to use men; an inability, mind you, not a refusal. On the contrary, when any of us volunteered or insisted upon taking responsibility off his shoulders he was delighted."

value to a row of ciphers, for his Cabinet, as a whole, was not composed of weak men. But the fact that the members of his Cabinet accepted implicitly his firm creed that the Cabinet ought to be an executive and not a political council, that it depended upon the President's policy, and that its main function should be merely to carry that policy into effect, gave to the public some justification for its belief that Wilson's was a "one-man" Government. This belief was further intensified by the President's extreme sensitiveness to hostile criticism, which more than anything else hindered frank interchange of opinion between himself and strong personalities. On more than one occasion he seemed to regard opposition as tantamount to personal hostility, an attitude which at times was not entirely unjustified. In the matter of minor appointments Wilson failed generally of success because he consistently refused to take a personal interest, leaving them to subordinates and admitting that political necessities must go far to determine the choice. Even in such an important problem as the appointment of the Peace Commission the President seems to have made his selection almost at haphazard. Many of his war appointments proved ultimately to be wise. But it is noteworthy that such men as Garfield, Baruch, and McCormick, who amply justified their choice, were appointed because Wilson knew personally their capacity and not because of previous success along special lines which would entitle them to public confidence.

The obstinacy of the President has become proverbial. The square chin, unconsciously protruded in argument, indicates definitely his capacity, as a British critic has put it, "to dig his toes in and hold on." On matters of method, however, where a basic principle is not involved, he is flexible. According as you approve or disapprove of him, he is "capable of development" or "inconsistent." Thus he completely changed front on the question of preparedness from 1914 to 1916. When the question of the initiative and referendum arose in Oregon, his attitude was the reverse of what it had been as professor of politics. When matters of detail are under discussion, he has displayed much willingness for and some skill in compromise, as was abundantly illustrated at Paris. But when he thinks that a principle is at stake, he prefers to accept any consequences, no matter how disastrous to his policy; witness his refusal to accept the Lodge reservation on Article X of the League Covenant.

All those included within the small circle of Wilson's intimates attest the charm and magnetism of his personality. The breadth of his reading is reflected in his conversation, which is enlivened by anecdotes that illustrate his points effectively and illumined by a sense of humor which some of his friends regard as his most salient trait. His manner is marked by extreme courtesy and, in view of the fixity of his opinions, a surprising lack of abruptness or dogmatism. But he has never been able to capitalize such personal advantages in his political relations. Apart from his intimates he is shy and reserved. The antithesis of Roosevelt, who loved to meet new individualities, Wilson has the college professor's shrinking from social contacts, and is not at ease in the presence of those with whom he is not familiar. Naturally, therefore, he lacks completely Roosevelt's capacity to make friends, and there is in him no trace of his predecessor's power to find exactly the right compliment for the right person. Under Roosevelt the White House opened its doors to every one who could bring the President anything of interest, whether in the field of science, literature, politics, or sport; and the Chief Magistrate, no matter who his guest, instantly found a common ground for discussion. That capacity Wilson did not possess. Furthermore his health was precarious and he was physically incapable of carrying the burden of the constant interviews that characterized the life of his immediate predecessors in the presidential office. He lived the life of a recluse and rarely received any one but friends of the family at the White House dinner table.)

While he thus saved himself from the social intercourse which for Roosevelt was a relaxation but which for him would have proved a nervous and physical drain, Wilson deprived himself of the political advantages that might have been derived from more extensive hospitality. He was unable to influence Congressmen except by reason of his authority as head of the party or nation. He lost many a chance of removing political opposition through the personal appeal which is so flattering and effective. He seems to have thought that if his policy was right in itself, Congressmen ought to vote for it, without the satisfaction of personal arguments, a singular misappreciation of human nature. The same was true of his relations with the Washington correspondents; he was never able to establish a man to man basis of intercourse. This incapacity in the vital matter of human contacts was, perhaps, his greatest political weakness. If he had been able to arouse warm personal devotion in his followers, if he could have inflamed them with enthusiasm such as that inspired by Roosevelt, rather than mere admiration, Wilson would have found his political task immeasurably lightened. It is not surprising that his mistakes in tactics should have been so numerous. His isolation and dependence upon tactical advisers, such as Tumulty and Burleson, lacking broad vision, led him into serious errors, most of which — such as his appeal for a Democratic Congress in 1918, his selection of the personnel of the Peace Commission, his refusal to compromise with the "mild reservationist Senators" in the summer of 1919 — were committed, significantly, when he was not in immediate contact with Colonel House.

The political strength of Wilson did not result primarily from intellectual power. His mind is neither profound nor subtle. His serious writings are sound but not characterized by originality, nor in his policies is there anything to indicate creative genius. He thinks straight and possesses the ability to concentrate on a single line of effort. He is skillful in catching an idea and adapting it to his purposes. Combined with his power of expression and his talent for making phrases, such qualities were of great assistance to him. But the real strength of the President lay rather in his gift of sensing what the common people wanted and his ability to put it into words for them. Few of his speeches are great; many of them are marred by tactless phrases, such as "too proud to fight" and "peace without victory." But nearly all of them express honestly the desires of the masses. His strength in New Jersey and the extraordinary effect produced in Europe by his war speeches might be cited as evidence of this peculiar power. He sought above everything to catch the trend of inarticulate rather than vociferous opinion. If one objects that his patience under German outrages was not truly representative, we must remember that opinion was slow in crystallizing, that his policy was endorsed by the election of 1916, and that when he finally advocated war in April, 1917, the country entered the struggle practically a unit.

But it is obvious that, however much political strength was assured the President by his instinctive appreciation of popular feeling, this was largely offset by the *gaucherie* of his political tactics. He had a genius for alienating persons who should have supported him and who agreed in general with the broad lines of his policies. Few men in public life have so thoroughly aroused the dislike of "the man in the street." Admitting that much of Wilson's unpopularity resulted from misunderstanding, from the feeling that he was a different sort, perhaps a "highbrow," the degree of dislike felt for him becomes almost inexplicable in the case of a President who, from all the evidence, was willing to sacrifice everything for what he considered to be the benefit of the common man. He might almost repeat Robespierre's final bitter and puzzled phrase: "To die for the people and to be abhorred by them." So keen was the irritation aroused by Wilson's methods and personality that many a citizen stated frankly that he preferred to see Wilsonian policies which he approved meet defeat, rather than see them carried to success by Wilson. This executive failing of the President was destined to jeopardize the greatest of his policies and to result in the personal tragedy of Wilson himself.

Certain large political principles stand out in Wilson's writings and career as Governor and President. Of these the most striking, perhaps, is his conviction that the President of the United States must be something more than a mere executive superintendent. The entire responsibility for the administration of government, he believed, should rest upon the President, and in order to meet that responsibility, he must keep the reins of control in his own hands. In his first essays and in his later writings Wilson expressed his disgust with the system of congressional committees which threw enormous power into the hands of irresponsible professional politicians, and called for a President who would break that system and exercise greater directive authority. For a time he seemed, under the influence of Bagehot, to have believed in the feasibility of introducing something like the parliamentary system into the government of the United States. To the last he regarded the President as a sort of Prime Minister, at the head of his party in the Legislature and able to count absolutely upon its loyalty. More than this, he believed that the President should take a large share of responsibility for the legislative programme and ought to push this programme through by all means at his disposal. Such a creed appeared in his early writings and was largely carried into operation during his administration. We find him bringing all possible pressure upon the New Jersey Legislature in order to redeem his campaign pledges. When elected President, he went directly to Congress with his message, instead of sending it to be read. Time and again he intervened to forward his special legislative interests by direct influence.

Both in his writings and in his actions Wilson has always advocated government by party. Theoretically and in practice he has been opposed to coalition government, for, in his belief, it divides responsibility. Although by no means an advocate of the old-type spoils system, rewards for party service seem to him essential. Curiously enough, while insisting that the President is the leader of his party like a Prime Minister, he has also described him, with an apparent lack of logic, as the leader of the country. Because Wilson has thus confused party and people, it is easy to understand why he has at times claimed to represent the nation when, in reality, he was merely representing partisan views. Such an attitude is naturally irritating to the Opposition and explains something of the virulence that characterized the attacks made upon him in 1918 and later.

Wilson's political sentiments are tinged by a constant and intense interest in the common man. More than once he has insisted that it was more important to know what was said by the fireside than what was said in the council chamber. His strongest political weapon, he believes, has been the appeal over the heads of politicians to public opinion. His dislike of cliques and his strong prejudice against anything that savors of special privilege shone clear in his attack upon the Princeton club system, and the same light has not infrequently dazzled his vision as President. Thus, while by no means a radical, he instinctively turned to the support of labor in its struggles with capital because of the abuse of its privilege by capital in the past and regardless of more recent abuse of its power by labor. Similarly at the Peace Conference his sympathies were naturally with every weak state and every minority group.

Such tendencies may have been strengthened by the intensity of his religious convictions. There have been few men holding high office in recent times so deeply and constantly affected by Christian faith as Woodrow Wilson. The son of a clergyman and subjected during his early years to the most lively and devout sort of Presbyterianism, he preserved in his own family circle, in later years, a similar atmosphere. Nor was his conviction of the immanence and spiritual guidance of the Deity ever divorced from his professional and public life.

We can discover in his presidential speeches many indications of his belief that the duties he had undertaken were laid upon him by God and that he might not deviate from what seemed to him the straight and appointed path. There is something reminiscent of Calvin in the stern and unswerving determination not to compromise for the sake of ephemeral advantage. This aspect of Wilson has been caught by a British critic, J. M. Keynes, who describes the President as a Nonconformist minister, whose thought and temperament were essentially theological, not intellectual, "with all the strength and weakness of that manner of thought, feeling, and expression." The observation is exact, although it does not in itself completely explain Wilson. Certainly nothing could be more characteristic of the President than the text of a Baccalaureate sermon which he preached at Princeton in 1907: "And be ye not conformed to this world." He believed with intensity that each individual must set up for himself a moral standard, which he must rigidly maintain regardless of the opinions of the community.

Entirely natural, therefore, is the emphasis which he has placed, whether as President of Princeton or of the United States, upon moral rather than material virtues. This, indeed, has been the essence of his political idealism. Such an emphasis has been for him at once a source of political strength and of weakness. The moralist unquestionably secures wide popular support; but he also wearies his audience, and many a voter has turned from Wilson in the spirit that led the Athenian to vote for the ostracism of Aristides, because he was tired of hearing him called "the Just." Whatever the immediate political effects, the country owes to Wilson a debt, which historians will doubtless acknowledge, for his insistence that morality must go hand in hand with public policy, that as with individuals, so with governments, true greatness is won by service rather than by acquisition, by sacrifice rather than by aggression. Wilson and Treitschke are at opposite poles.

During his academic career Wilson seems to have displayed little interest in foreign affairs, and his knowledge of European politics, although sufficient for him to produce an admirable handbook on governments, including foreign as well as our own, was probably not profound. During his first year in the White House, he was typical of the Democratic party, which then approved the political isolation of the United States, abhorred the kind of commercial imperialism summed up in the phrase "dollar diplomacy," and apparently believed that the essence of foreign policy was to keep one's own hands clean. The development of Wilson from this parochial point of view to one which centers his whole being upon a policy of unselfish international service, forms, to a large extent, the main thread of the narrative which follows.

CHAPTER II

NEUTRALITY

DESPITE the wars and rumors of wars in Europe
after 1910, few Americans perceived the gathering
of the clouds, and probably not one in ten thousand
felt more than an ordinary thrill of interest on the
morning of June 29, 1914, when they read that the
Archduke Franz Ferdinand of Austria had been
assassinated. Nor, a month later, when it became
obvious that the resulting crisis was to precipitate
another war in the Balkans, did most Americans
realize that the world was hovering on the brink of
momentous events. Not even when the most dire
forebodings were realized and the great powers of
Europe were drawn into the quarrel, could America
appreciate its significance. Crowds gazed upon the
bulletin boards and tried to picture the steady
advance of German field-gray through the streets
of Liège, asked their neighbors what were these
French 75's, and endeavored to locate Mons and

Verdun on inadequate maps. Interest could not be more intense, but it was the interest of the moving-picture devotee. Even the romantic voyage of the *Kronprinzessin Cecilie* with her cargo of gold, seeking to elude the roving British cruisers, seemed merely theatrical. It was a tremendous show and we were the spectators. Only the closing of the Stock Exchange lent an air of reality to the crisis.

It was true that the Spanish War had made of the United States a world power, but so firmly rooted in American minds was the principle of complete political isolation from European affairs that the typical citizen could not imagine any cataclysm on the other side of the Atlantic so engrossing as to engage the active participation of his country. The whole course of American history had deepened the general feeling of aloofness from Europe and heightened the effect of the advice given by the first President when he warned the country to avoid entangling alliances. In the early nineteenth century the United States was a country apart, for in the days when there was neither steamship nor telegraph the Atlantic in truth separated the New World from the Old. After the close of the "second war of independence," in 1815, the possibility of foreign complications seemed remote. The attention of the young nation was directed to domestic concerns, to the building up of manufactures, to the extension of the frontiers westward. The American nation turned its back to the Atlantic. There was a steady and welcome stream of immigrants from Europe, but there was little speculation or interest as to its headwaters.

Governmental relations with European states were disturbed at times by crises of greater or less importance. The proximity of the United States to and interest in Cuba compelled the Government to recognize the political existence of Spain; a French army was ordered out of Mexico when it was felt to be a menace; the presence of immigrant Irish in large numbers always gave a note of uncertainty to the national attitude towards Great Britain. The export of cotton from the Southern States created industrial relations of such importance with Great Britain that, during the Civil War, after the establishment of the blockade on the Confederate coast, wisdom and forbearance were needed on both sides to prevent the breaking out of armed conflict. But during the last third of the century, which was marked in this country by an extraordinary industrial evolution and an increased interest in domestic administrative issues, the attitude of the United States towards Europe, except during the brief Venezuelan crisis and the war with Spain, was generally characterized by the indifference which is the natural outcome of geographical separation.

In diplomatic language American foreign policy, so far as Europe was concerned, was based upon the principle of "non-intervention." The right to manage their affairs in their own way without interference was conceded to European Governments and a reciprocal attitude was expected of them. The American Government followed strictly the purpose of not participating in any political arrangements made between European states regarding European issues. Early in the life of the nation Jefferson had correlated the double aspect of this policy: "Our first and fundamental maxim," he said, "should be never to entangle ourselves in the broils of Europe; our second, never to suffer Europe to intermeddle with cis-Atlantic affairs." The influence of John Quincy Adams crystallized this double policy in the Monroe Doctrine, which, as compensation for denying to European states the right to intervene in American politics, sacrificed the generous sympathies of many Americans, among them

President Monroe himself, with the republican movements across the Atlantic. With the continued and increasing importance of the Monroe Doctrine as a principle of national policy, the natural and reciprocal aspect of that doctrine, implying political isolation from Europe, became more deeply imbedded in the national consciousness.

There was, it is true, another aspect to American foreign policy besides the European, namely, that concerning the Pacific and the Far East, which, as diplomatic historians have pointed out, does not seem to have been affected by the tradition of isolation. Since the day when the western frontier was pushed to the Golden Gate, the United States has taken an active interest in problems of the Pacific. Alaska was purchased from Russia. An American seaman was the first to open the trade of Japan to the outside world and thus precipitated the great revolution which has touched every aspect of Far Eastern questions. American traders watched carefully the commercial development of Oriental ports, in which Americans have played an active rôle. In China and in the maintenance of the open door especially, has America taken the keenest interest. It is a matter of pride that American policy, always of a purely commercial and peaceful nature, showed itself less aggressive than that of some European states. But the Government insisted upon the recognition of American interest in every Far Eastern issue that might be raised, and was ready to intervene with those of Europe in moments of crisis or danger.

A fairly clear-cut distinction might thus be made between American pretensions in the different parts of the world. In the Americas the nation claimed that sort of preëminence which was implied by the Monroe Doctrine, a preëminence which as regards the Latin-American states north of the Orinoco many felt must be actively enforced, in view of special interests in the Caribbean. In the Far East the United States claimed an equality of status with the European powers. In the rest of the world, Europe, Africa, the Levant, the traditional American policy of abstention held good absolutely, at least until the close of the century.

The war with Spain affected American foreign policy vitally. The holding of the Philippines, even if it were to prove merely temporary, created new relations with all the great powers, of Europe as of Asia; American Caribbean interests were strengthened; and the victory over a European power, even one of a second class in material strength, necessarily altered the traditional attitude of the nation towards the other states of Europe and theirs towards it. This change was stimulated by the close attention which American merchants and bankers began to give to European combinations and policies, particularly to the exploitation of thinly populated districts by European states. Even before the Spanish War a keen-sighted student of foreign affairs, Richard Olney, had declared that the American people could not assume an attitude of indifference towards European politics and that the hegemony of a single continental state would be disastrous to their prosperity if not to their safety. Conversely Europeans began to watch America with greater care. The victory over Spain was resented and the fear of American commercial development began to spread. The Kaiser had even talked of a continental customs union to meet American competition. On the other hand, Great Britain, which had displayed a benevolent attitude during the Spanish War and whose admiral at Manila had perhaps blocked German interference, showed an increasing desire for a close understanding. The friendship of the United States, itself once a British dependency, for the British colonies was natural and

American interests in the Far East had much in common with those of Great Britain.

External evidence of the new place of the United States in the world might be found in the position taken by Roosevelt as peacemaker between Russia and Japan, and, more significantly, in the rôle played by the American representative, Henry White, at the Conference of Algeciras in 1906. Not merely did the American Government consent to discuss matters essentially European in character, but its attitude proved almost decisive in the settlement then drafted. It is true that the Senate, in approving that settlement, refused to assume responsibility for its maintenance and reiterated its adherence to traditional policy. But those who watched developments with intelligent eyes must have agreed with Roosevelt when he said: "We have no choice, we people of the United States, as to whether we shall play a great part in the affairs of the world. That has been decided for us by fate, by the march of events." Yet it may be questioned whether the average American, during the first decade of the twentieth century, realized the change that had come over relations with Europe. The majority of citizens certainly felt that anything happening east of the Atlantic was none of their business, just as everything that occurred in the Americas was entirely outside the scope of European interference.

There is little to show that Woodrow Wilson, at the time when he entered upon his duties as President, was one of the few Americans who fully appreciated the new international position of the United States and its consequences, even had there been no war. The Democratic platform of 1912 hardly mentioned foreign policy, and Wilson's Inaugural contained no reference to anything except domestic matters. Certain problems inherited from the previous Administration forced upon the President, however, the formulation, if not of a policy, at least of an attitude. The questions of the Panama Canal tolls and Japanese immigration, the Mexican situation, the Philippines, general relations with Latin-America, all demanded attention. In each case Wilson displayed a willingness to sacrifice, a desire to avoid stressing the material strength of the United States, an anxiety to compromise, which matched in spirit the finest traditions of American foreign policy, which has generally been marked by high ideals. Many of his countrymen, possibly without adequate study or command of the facts, supposed that Wilson was

inspired less by positive ideals than by the belief
that no problem of a foreign nature was worth a
quarrel. People liked the principle contained in the
sentence: "We can afford to exercise the self-re-
straint of a really great nation which realizes its own
strength and scorns to misuse it." But they also
wondered whether the passivity of the Government
did not in part proceed from the fact that the President could not make up his mind what he wanted
to do. They looked upon his handling of the Mexican situation as clear evidence of a lack of policy.
Nevertheless the country as a whole, without ex-
pressing enthusiasm for Wilson's attitude, was
obviously pleased by his attempts to avoid foreign entanglements, and in the early summer of
1914 the eyes of the nation were focused upon
domestic issues.

Then came the war in Europe.

Today, after the long years of stress and
struggle in which the crimes of Germany have received full advertisement, few Americans will admit that they did not perceive during that first
week of August, 1914, the complete significance of
the moral issues involved in the European war.
They read back into their thoughts of those early

days the realization which, in truth, came only later, that Germany was the brutal aggressor attacking those aspects of modern civilization which are dear to America. In fact there were not many then who grasped the essential truth that the cause defended by Great Britain and France was indeed that of America and that their defeat would bring the United States face to face with vital danger, both material and moral.

Partisanship, of course, was not lacking and frequently it was of an earnest kind; in view of the large number of European-born who enjoyed citizenship, sympathy with one side or the other was inevitably warm. West of the Mississippi it was some time before the masses were stirred from their indifference to and their ignorance of the struggle. But on the Atlantic seaboard and in the Middle West opinion became sharply divided. The middle-class German-Americans naturally espoused with some vehemence the justice of the Fatherland's cause. German intellectuals of influence, such as Hugo Münsterberg, inveighed against the hypocrisy and the decadence of the Entente powers. Many Americans who had lived or had been educated in Germany, some professors who had been brought into contact with the Kaiser, explained the "essentially defensive character" of Germany's struggle against the threatening Slav. Certain of the politically active Irish elements, anxious to discredit the British, also lent their support to the German cause.

On the Atlantic coast, however, the general trend of opinion ran strongly in favor of the Entente. The brave defense of the Belgians at Liège against terrible odds evoked warm sympathy; the stories of the atrocities committed by the invading Germans, constantly more frequent and more brutal in character, enhanced that feeling. The valorous retreat of the French and their last-ditch stand on the Marne compelled admiration. Moreover, the school histories of the United States with their emphasis upon La Fayette and the aid given by the French in the first fight for liberty proved to be of no small importance in the molding of sympathy. Business men naturally favored Great Britain, both because of financial relationships and because of their dislike and fear of German commercial methods.

But in all this partisanship there was little appreciation of the peril that might result from German victory and no articulate demand that the United States intervene. Warm sympathy might be given to one side or the other, but the almost universal opinion was that the war was none of our business. Even Theodore Roosevelt, who later was to be one of the most determined advocates of American intervention on the side of the Entente, writing for *The Outlook* in September, 1914, congratulated the country on its separation from European quarrels, which made possible the preservation of our peace.

Whatever the trend of public opinion, President Wilson would have insisted upon neutrality. Everything in his character and policy demanded the maintenance of peace. He had entered office with a broad programme of social reform in view, and the attainment of his ideals depended upon domestic tranquillity. He was, furthermore, a real pacifist, believing that war is debasing morally and disastrous economically. Finally, he was convinced that the United States was consecrated to a special task, namely, the inspiration of politics by moral factors; if the nation was to accomplish this task its example must be a higher example than one of force. Unquestionably he looked forward to acting as mediator in the struggle and thus securing for the country and himself new prestige such as had come in Roosevelt's mediation between

Russia and Japan. But the main thought in his mind was, first, the preservation of peace for the sake of peace; and next, to attain the supreme glory of showing the world that greatness and peaceableness are complementary in national character and not antithetic. "We are champions of peace and of concord," he said, "and we should be very jealous of this distinction which we have sought to earn."

Wilson's determination was strengthened by his obvious failure to distinguish between the war aims of the two sides. He did not at first see the moral issue involved. He was anxious to "reserve judgment until the end of the war, when all its events and circumstances can be seen in their entirety and in their true relations." When appeals and protests were sent to him from Germany, Belgium, and France dealing with infractions of the law and practice of nations, he was willing to return a response to Germany, which had confessedly committed an international wrong, identical with that sent to Belgium which had suffered from that wrong. Wilson has himself confessed that "America did not at first see the full meaning of the war. It looked like a natural raking out of the pent-up jealousies and rivalries of the complicated politics of Europe. . . . We, at the distance of America, looked on at first without a full comprehension of what the plot was getting into." [1] That the aims of the belligerent powers might affect the conscience or the fortunes of America he did not perceive. He urged us not to be "thrown off our balance by a war with which we have nothing to do, whose causes cannot touch us, whose very existence affords us opportunities of friendship and disinterested service which should make us ashamed of any thought of hostility or fearful preparation for trouble." Hence his proclamation of neutrality, which was universally accepted as right. Hence, also, his adjuration to be "impartial in thought as well as in action," which was not so universally accepted and marks, perhaps, a definite rift between Wilson and the bulk of educated opinion in the Northeast.

During the early days of August Wilson had proclaimed his desire to act as mediator between the warring forces, although he must have realized that the suggestion would prove fruitless at that moment. Again, after the battle of the Marne, he took advantage of German discouragement, apparently receiving a hint from Johann von

[1] Speech on the *George Washington*, July 4, 1919.

Bernstorff, German Ambassador in Washington, to sound the belligerents on the possibility of an arrangement. Failing a second time to elicit serious consideration of peace, he withdrew to wait for a better opportunity. Thus the .Germans, beaten back from Paris, vainly pounded the allied lines on the Yser; the Russians, after forcing their path through Galicia, defended Warsaw with desperation; while Wilson kept himself and his country strictly aloof from the conflict.

But no mere desires or declarations could prevent the war from touching America, and each day made more apparent the difficulties and the dangers of neutrality. The Atlantic no longer separated the two worlds. In September and October the British Government, taking advantage of the naval supremacy assured by their fleet, issued Orders in Council designed to provide for close control of neutral commerce and to prevent the importation of contraband into Germany. British supervision of war-time trade has always been strict and its interpretation of the meaning of contraband broad; the present instance was no exception. American ships and cargoes were seized and confiscated to an extent which, while it doubtless seemed justified to the British, who were fighting for their lives, evoked a chorus of bitter complaints from American producers and exporters. Commerce with neutral countries of Europe threatened to become completely interrupted. On the 21st of October and again on the 26th of December, the State Department sent notes of protest to the British Government. The tone of the discussion was notably sharpened by the seizure of the *Wilhelmina*, supposedly an American ship, though, as later developed, she had been chartered by a German agent in New York, Dr. Heinrich F. Albert, in order to bring the Anglo-American dispute to a head.

How far the interference with our trade by the British might have embittered relations, if other issues had not seemed more pressing, no one can say. Precisely at the moment when business men were beginning to call upon Wilson for a sturdier defense of American commercial rights, a controversy with Germany eclipsed, at least from the eye of the general public, all other foreign questions. From the moment when the defeat on the Marne showed the Germans that victory was not likely to come quickly to their arms, the Berlin Government realized the importance of preventing the export of American munitions. Since the allies held control of the seas an embargo on such export would be entirely to German advantage, and the head of German propaganda in this country, a former Colonial Secretary, Dr. Bernhard Dernburg, attempted to mobilize German-American sentiment and to bring pressure upon Congressmen through their constituents in favor of such an embargo. It was easy to allege that the export of arms, since they went to the allied camp alone, was on its face, unneutral. Several Senators approved the embargo, among them the chairman of the Senate Foreign Relations Committee, William J. Stone of Missouri. Against the proposed embargo Wilson set his face steadfastly. He perceived the fallacy of the German argument and insisted that to prevent the export of arms would be itself unneutral. The inability of the Central Powers to import arms from the United States resulted from their inferiority on the high seas; the Government would be departing from its position of impartiality if it failed to keep American markets open to every nation of the world, belligerent or neutral. The United States could not change the rules in the middle of the game for the advantage of one side. The perfect legality of Wilson's decision has been frankly recognized since the war by the German Ambassador.

But the execution of German military plans demanded that the allied shortage in munitions, upon which the Teutons counted for success in the spring campaigns, should not be replenished from American sources. Failing to budge Wilson on the proposal of an embargo, they launched themselves upon a more reckless course. On February 4, 1915, the German Admiralty issued a proclamation to the effect that after the 18th of February, German submarines would destroy every enemy merchant vessel found in the waters about the British Isles, which were declared a "war zone"; and that it might not be possible to provide for the safety of crew or passengers of destroyed vessels. Neutral ships were warned of the danger of destruction if they entered the zone. The excuse alleged for this decided departure from the custom of nations was the British blockade upon foodstuffs, which had been declared as a result of the control of food in Germany by the Government. Here was quite a different matter from British interference with American trade-rights; for if the German threat were carried into effect it signified not merely the destruction or loss of property, for which restitution might be made, but the possible drowning of American citizens, perhaps women and children, who would be entirely within their rights in traveling upon merchant vessels and to whom the Government owed protection.

Wilson's reply was prompt and definite. "If the commanders of German vessels of war should . . . destroy on the high seas an American vessel or the lives of American citizens, it would be difficult for the Government of the United States to view the act in any other light than as an indefensible violation of neutral rights. . . . The Government of the United States would be constrained to hold the Imperial German Government to a strict accountability for such acts of their naval authorities and to take any steps it might be necessary to take to safeguard American lives and property and to secure to American citizens the full enjoyment of their acknowledged rights on the high seas." It was the clearest of warnings. Would Germany heed it? And if she did not, would Wilson surrender his pacific ideals and take the nation into war?

CHAPTER III

THE SUBMARINE

EARLY in the winter of 1914–1915 President Wilson apparently foresaw something of the complications likely to arise from the measures and counter-measures taken by the belligerents to secure control of overseas commerce, and sent his personal adviser, Colonel House, across the Atlantic to study the possibilities of reaching a *modus vivendi*. There was no man so well qualified for the mission. Edward Mandell House was a Texan by birth, but a cosmopolitan by nature. His hobby was practical politics; his avocation the study of history and government. His catholicity of taste is indicated by the nature of his library, which includes numerous volumes not merely on the social sciences but also on philosophy and poetry. His intellectual background was thus no less favorable than his political for the post which he assumed as Wilson's personal adviser   Disqualified by physical delicacy from entering the political arena himself and consistently refusing office, he had for years controlled the political stage in his own State; in 1912, exercising strong influence in the national party organization, he had done much to crystallize sentiment in favor of Wilson as presidential candidate. Slight in stature, quiet in manner and voice, disliking personal publicity, with an almost uncanny instinct for divining the motives that actuate men, he possessed that which Wilson lacked — the capacity to "mix," to meet his fellow mortals, no matter what their estate, on a common ground.

Courteous and engaging, Colonel House was an unexcelled negotiator: he had a genius for compromise, as perfect a control of his emotions as of his facial expression, and a pacific magnetism that soothed into reasonableness the most heated interlocutor. His range of acquaintance in the United States was unparalleled. Abroad, previous to the war, he had discussed international relations with the Kaiser and the chief statesmen of France and England. His experience of American politics and knowledge of foreign affairs, whether derived from men or from books, were matched by an almost unerring penetration in the analysis of a political situation, domestic or European. As a liberal idealist and pacifist, he saw eye to eye with Wilson; his sense of political actualities, however, was infinitely more keen.

But even the skill of Colonel House was not sufficient to induce Germany to hold her hand, and, as spring advanced, it became increasingly clear that she was resolved to carry her threats of unrestricted submarine warfare into effect. The quality of Wilson's pacifism was about to be put to the test. In March a British steamer, the *Falaba*, was sunk and an American citizen drowned; some weeks later an American boat, the *Cushing*, was attacked by a German airplane; and on the 1st of May, another American steamer, the *Gulflight*, was sunk by a submarine with the loss of two American lives. When was Wilson going to translate into action his summary warning of "strict accountability?" Even as the question was asked, we heard that the Germans had sunk the *Lusitania*. On the 7th of May, 1915, at two in the afternoon, the pride of the British merchant marine was struck by two torpedoes fired from a German submarine. She sank in half an hour. More than eleven hundred of her passengers and crew were drowned, among them one hundred and twenty-four Americans, men, women, and children.

The cry that went up from America was one of anguish, but still more one of rage. This attack upon non-combatant travelers, citizens of a neutral state, had been callously premeditated and ruthlessly executed in cold blood. The German Government had given frigid warning, in a newspaper advertisement, of its intention to affront the custom of nations and the laws of humanity. A wave of the bitterest anti-German feeling swept down the Atlantic coast and out to the Mississippi; for the first time there became apparent a definite trend of opinion demanding the entrance of the United States into the war on the side of the Entente. On that day Wilson might have won a declaration of war, so strong was popular sentiment; and despite the comparative indifference of the Missouri valley and the Far West, he might have aroused enthusiasm if not unity.

But a declaration of war then would, in all probability, have been a mistake. Entrance into the war at that time would have been based upon neither judgment nor ideals, but merely upon emotion. The American people were in no way prepared to bring material aid to the cause of justice, nor did the nation yet appreciate the moral issues involved. It would have been a war of revenge for American lives lost. / The President was by temperament disinclined to listen to the passionate demands for intervention, and, as historian, he must have had in mind the error committed by McKinley when he permitted the declaration of war on Spain, after the sinking of the *Maine* in 1898. Sober afterthought has generally agreed that Wilson was right. But he was himself led into a serious error that produced consequences which were not soon to be dissipated. Speaking three days after the event, when the world looked to him to express the soul of America, and dealing with the spirit of Americanism, he permitted an unfortunate phrase to enter his address and to cloud his purpose. "There is such a thing," he said, "as a man being too proud to fight." The phrase was by no means essential to the main points of his address; it was preceded by one of greater importance, namely that "the example of America must be a special example . . . of peace because peace is the healing and elevating influence of the world and strife is not." / It was followed by another of equal importance, that a nation may be so much in the right "that it does not need to convince others by force that it is right." These two phrases expressed what was in the President's mind clearly and definitely: the United States was consecrated to ideals which could not be carried into effect through force, unless every other method dictated by supreme patience had failed. But the world did not notice them. All that it remembered was that the United States was "too proud to fight." What did this mean to the average man except that the country was afraid to fight? The peoples of the Entente powers were contemptuous; Germans were reassured; Americans were humiliated.

Wilson the phrase-maker was betrayed by a phrase, and it was to pursue him like a Fury. The chorus of indignation and shame aroused by this phrase covered completely the determination and skill with which he entered upon the diplomatic struggle with Germany. His purpose was definite. He had gone on record in February that the United States Government would protect the rights of American citizens, and he was bound to secure from Germany a promise that merchant ships should not be torpedoed without warning or assuring the lives of crew and passengers. And yet by virtue of his pacific principles this promise could not be forcibly extracted until every other possible method had been attempted in vain. Unquestionably he was supported in his policy by many, perhaps most, thoughtful people, although wherever support was given him in the East it was generally grudging. Such a representative and judicial mind as that of ex-President Taft favored cool consideration and careful action. But the difficulties encountered by the President were tremendous. On the one hand he met the bitter denunciations of the group, constantly increasing in numbers, which demanded our immediate intervention on the side of the Entente. Led by Roosevelt, who no longer felt as in the previous September, that the United States had no immediate interest in the war, this group included influential men of business and many writers. They had lost patience with Wilson's patience. His policy was, in their opinion, that of a coward. On the other hand, Wilson was assailed by pro-Germans and die-hard pacifists; the former believed that the British blockade justified Germany's submarine warfare; the latter were afraid even of strong language in diplomatic notes, lest it lead to war. At the very outset of the diplomatic controversy with Germany, before the second *Lusitania* note was dispatched, the Secretary of State, William Jennings Bryan, resigned, in the belief that the President's tone was too peremptory. For Bryan was willing to arbitrate even Germany's right to drown American citizens on the high seas. The defection of this influential politician a year previous would have weakened Wilson seriously, but by now the President had won secure control of the party. He was, indeed, strengthened diplomatically by Bryan's resignation, as the latter, in a conversation with the Austrian Ambassador, had given the impression that American protests need not be taken overseriously. His continuance in office might have encouraged German leaders to adopt a bolder tone.

From the very beginning of his attempts to obtain from Germany a disavowal for the sinking of the *Lusitania* and a promise not to sink without warning, the President took his stand upon high ground. Not merely did he insist upon the rights guaranteed to neutrals by the law of nations; he took the controversy out of the class of ordinary subjects of diplomatic discussion and contended "for nothing less high and sacred than the rights of humanity." To this he recurred in each of his notes. Germany avoided the issue. At first she insisted that the *Lusitania* was armed, carrying explosives of war, transporting troops from Canada, and thus virtually acting as a naval auxiliary. After the falsity of this assertion was shown, she adduced the restrictions placed by Great Britain

He sent notes to Germany

on neutral trade as excuse for submarine operations, and contended that the circumstances of naval warfare in the twentieth century had so changed that the principles of international law no longer held good.

Each time Wilson returned to his point that the "rights of neutrals are based upon principle, not upon expediency, and the principles are immutable. Illegal and inhuman acts . . . are manifestly indefensible when they deprive neutrals of their acknowledged rights, particularly when they violate the right to life itself. If a belligerent cannot retaliate against an enemy without injuring the lives of neutrals, as well as their property, humanity, as well as justice and a due regard for the dignity of neutral powers should dictate that the practice be discontinued." Wilson terminated his third note to Germany with a warning, which had the tone, if not the form, of an ultimatum; there must be a scrupulous observance of neutral rights in this critical matter, as repetition of "acts in contravention of those rights must be regarded by the Government of the United States, when they affect American citizens, as deliberately unfriendly."

The exchange of notes consumed much time and proved a severe test for American patience. The first *Lusitania* note was sent on the 13th of May and it was not until the 1st of September that the German Government finally gave a pledge that was acceptable to Wilson. In the meantime there had been continued sinkings, or attempts to sink, in clear violation of the principles for which the President was contending. The *Nebraskan*, the *Armenian*, the *Orduna*, were subjected to submarine attacks. On the 19th of August the *Arabic* was sunk and two Americans lost. The ridicule heaped upon the President by the British and certain sections of the American press, for his writing of diplomatic notes, was only equaled by the sense of humiliation experienced by pro-Entente elements in this country. *Punch* issued a cartoon in which Uncle Sam pointed to Wilson as having outstripped the record made by Job for patience. Nevertheless Wilson obtained the main point for which he was striving. On September 1, 1915, the German Government gave the definite pledge that "Liners will not be sunk by our submarines without warning and without safety of the lives of non-combatants, provided that the liners do not try to escape or offer resistance." Wilson had sought to safeguard a principle by compelling from Germany a written acknowledgment of its validity. So much he had won and without the exercise of force. Even those whose nerves were most overwrought by the long-drawn-out negotiations, admitted that it was a diplomatic victory.

The victory was not clean-cut, for Germany had not yet disavowed the sinking of the *Lusitania,* nor did the category "liners" seem to include all merchant vessels. How real was even the partial victory remained to be seen. Within three days of the German pledge the *Hesperian* was sunk and an American citizen drowned. On the 7th of November the *Ancona* was torpedoed in the Mediterranean by an Austrian submarine with the loss of more American lives. It is true that after each case a disavowal was made and a renewal of promises vouchsafed. But it seemed obvious that Germany was merely playing for time and also that she counted upon pro-German and pacifist agitation in this country. For a brief period it appeared as if her hopes were not to be entirely disappointed. British merchant vessels, following long-established custom, had for some months been armed for purposes of defense. The German Government on February 10, 1916, announced that henceforward such armed merchantmen would be regarded as auxiliary cruisers and would be sunk without warning. It was

unfortunate that Robert Lansing, who had succeeded Bryan as Secretary of State, had proposed
on January 18, 1916, to the diplomatic representatives of the Allied forces that they cease the arming
of merchantmen as a means of securing from Germany a pledge which would cover all merchantmen
as well as passenger liners; this proposal gave to
Germany a new opportunity for raising the issue
of the submarine. But either Lansing's proposal
had been made without Mr. Wilson's sanction or
the President changed his mind, since on the 10th
of February Wilson declared that he intended to
recognize the right of merchantmen to arm for purposes of defense. Once more he insisted that the
rules of war could not be changed during war for
the advantage of one side.

His declaration led at once to something like a
revolt of Congress. Already some of those who
especially feared intervention had been suffering
from an attack of panic as a result of Wilson's recent decision to support the preparedness movement. They were further terrified by the possibility that some American citizen traveling on
an armed merchantman might lose his life and
that the demand for entrance into the war might
thus become irresistible. Bryanites, pro-German

propagandists, and Irish combined against the President, and were reinforced by all the discontented elements who hoped to break Wilson's control of the Democratic party. The combination seemed like a new cave of Adullam. Resolutions were introduced in the Senate by Thomas P. Gore and in the House by Jeff McLemore, based upon suggestions made by Bryan nine months before, that American citizens should be warned not to travel on armed merchant vessels. Senator Stone, of the Foreign Relations Committee, supported these resolutions and it appeared probable that Germany would find her strongest support in the American Congress.

Wilson struck sharply. Not merely his leadership of the party and the country was at stake, but also that moral leadership of neutral nations and the world toward which the struggle with Germany was to take him. Refusing to receive Senator Stone, he sent him a letter in which the cardinal points of his position were underlined. "Once accept a single abatement of right," he insisted, "and many other humiliations would certainly follow, and the whole fine fabric of international law might crumble under our hands piece by piece. What we are now contending for in this matter is the very essence of the things that have made America a sovereign nation. She cannot yield them without conceding her own impotency as a Nation and making virtual surrender of her independent position among the nations of the world." This definite enunciation was in effect an appeal to the American people, which came as a relief to those who had suffered from presidential patience under German outrages. The storm of public feeling aroused against the rebellious Congressmen was such that Wilson's victory became assured. Demanding concrete justification of his stand, he insisted that the resolutions be put to the vote. The issue was somewhat confused in the Senate so that the vote was not decisive; but in the House the McLemore resolution was defeated by a vote of 276 to 142.

And yet the submarine issue was not finally closed. Less than a month after the rights of American citizens were thus maintained, the British passenger steamer *Sussex*, crossing the English Channel, was torpedoed without warning. It was the clearest violation of the pledge given by the German Government the previous September. Once again Wilson acted without precipitancy. He waited until the Germans should present explanations and thereafter took more than a week in which to formulate his decision. Finally, on April 19, 1916, he called the two houses of Congress in joint session to lay before them his note to Germany. Unlike his *Lusitania* notes, this was a definite ultimatum, clearly warranted by the undeniable fact that Germany had broken a solemn pledge. After recounting the long list of events which had so sorely tried American patience, Wilson concluded that " unless the Imperial German Government should now immediately declare and effect an abandonment of its present methods of warfare against passenger and freight carrying vessels this Government can have no choice but to sever diplomatic relations with the Government of the German Empire altogether." The force of the ultimatum was emphasized by the general tone of the note, in which, as in the *Lusitania* notes, the President spoke not so much for the legal rights of the United States, as in behalf of the moral rights of all humanity. He stressed the "principles of humanity as embodied in the law of nations," and excoriated the "inhumanity of submarine warfare"; he terminated by stating that the United States would contemplate a diplomatic break with reluctance, but would feel constrained to take the step "in behalf of humanity and the rights of neutral nations." This note of emphasis upon America's duty to mankind rather than to herself formed the main theme of a speech delivered two days previous: "America will have forgotten her traditions whenever upon any occasion she fights merely for herself under such circumstances as will show that she has forgotten to fight for all mankind. And the only excuse that America can ever have for the assertion of her physical force is that she asserts it in behalf of the interests of humanity."

Germany yielded before Wilson's ultimatum, though with bad grace, and promised that no more merchant ships would be sunk "without warning and without saving human lives." But she also tried to make her promise conditional upon the cessation by Great Britain of methods of warfare which Germany called illegal, implying that her pledge might be withdrawn at her pleasure: "the German Government . . . must reserve itself complete liberty of action." This condition Wilson, in taking note of Germany's pledge, definitely waved aside: "the Government of the United States notifies the Imperial Government that it cannot for a moment entertain, much less discuss, a suggestion that respect by German naval authorities

for the rights of American citizens upon the high
seas should in any way or in the slightest degree be made contingent upon the conduct of any
other government affecting the rights of neutrals
and noncombatants. Responsibility in such matters is single, not joint; absolute, not relative."
By its silence the German Government seemed to
acquiesce and the crisis was over. The country
had been close to war, but intervention might yet
be avoided if Germany kept her word. That, however, was a condition upon which people were
learning not to rely.

It is obvious that by the early summer of 1916
President Wilson's attitude on foreign affairs had
undergone a notable transformation from that
parochial spirit of 1914 which had led him to declare that the war was no concern of America; he
had given over completely the tradition that if we
keep our own hands clean we fulfill our duty. He
had begun to elaborate an idealistic policy of service to the world, not unreminiscent of the altruis-
tic schemes of Clay and Webster for assisting op-
pressed republicans in Europe during the first third
of the nineteenth century. Wilson, like those
statesmen, had always felt that the position of the
United States in the world was of a special sort,

quite different from that of the European states, and circumstances were forcing him to take the stand that the nation must assume the lead in the world in order to ensure the operation of the principles that Americans believe in. "We are in some sort and by the force of circumstances the responsible spokesman of the rights of humanity." He still opposed active intervention in the war; the mission of the United States was a higher one than could adequately be fulfilled through war; the kind of service we could best give was not fighting. Yet he was brought to admit, even before the *Sussex* crisis (February 26, 1916), that in the last instance war might be necessary if the American people were to assume the rôle of champion of liberty in the world at large, as they had championed it in the Americas; for the rights of humanity must be made secure against menace: "America ought to keep out of this war . . . at the expense of everything except this single thing upon which her character and history are founded, her sense of humanity and justice. . . . Valor withholds itself from all small implications and entanglements and waits for the great opportunity, when the sword will flash as if it carried the light of heaven upon its blade." Thus the possibility of ultimate force was implied. Eighteen months previous, peace had been for Wilson an end in itself. Now it was subordinated to the greater end implied in maintaining the principle of justice in the world.

During this period popular sentiment also underwent a notable development. Americans reacted sharply to German threats and outrages, and were thrown off their comfortable balance by the events which touched American honor and safety so closely. Like Wilson, they were shaken out of that sense of isolation which enveloped them in 1914, and they were thus prepared for the reception of broader ideals. The process of education was slow and difficult. It was hampered by the confusion of foreign issues. Propagandists took advantage of the controversy with Great Britain in order to obscure the principles upon which the discussions with Germany were based. The increasing stringency of British control of commerce and the blacklisting of various American firms by the British authorities resulted in numerous American protests and to some warmth of feeling. Wilson was no particular friend of the British, but he rightly insisted upon the distinction between the dispute with Germany, which involved the common right of humanity to life, and that with Great Britain,

5

which involved merely rights of property. Nevertheless that distinction was blurred in the minds of many Americans, and their perception of the new ideals of foreign policy was necessarily confused.

The education of the American people to the significance of the issue was also hampered by the material change that came over the country during the latter part of 1915 and the spring of 1916. The influx of gold and the ease with which fortunes were accumulated could not but have widespread effects. The European war came at a moment when the United States was passing through a period of comparatively hard times. Stringency was naturally increased by the liquidation of foreign investments in 1914 and the closing of European markets to American commerce. Business was dull. But this condition was rapidly altered through the placing of large contracts by the Entente Governments and the most extensive buying by foreign purchasers. New markets were found among the neutral states, which were unable to buy in Europe. Naturally there developed a rapid extension of industrial activities. New manufacturing concerns grew up, large and small, as a result of these adventitious conditions, which paid enormous returns. Activities upon the stock market were unparalleled. New and sudden fortunes were made; millionaires became common. The whole world was debtor to America and a golden stream flowed across the Atlantic. Prices rose rapidly and wages followed.

Inevitably materialism conquered, at least for the moment. The demand for luxuries was only equaled by the craze for entertainment. Artisans and shopgirls invaded the jewelry stores of Fifth Avenue. Metropolitan life was a succession of luncheons and teas, where fertile brains were busied with the invention of new dancing steps rather than the issues of the European war. Cabarets were crowded and seats for midnight beauty shows must be secured well in advance or by means of gargantuan tips to plutocratic head waiters. Much of the materialism was simply external. In every town American women by the thousand gave lavishly of their time and strength to knit and roll bandages for the fighters and wounded overseas. America was collecting millions for the relief of Belgium, Serbia, and for the Red Cross. The American Ambulance in France was served by men imbued with the spirit of sacrifice. Thousands of American youths enlisted in the Canadian forces. The general atmosphere of the country, however, was heavy with amusement and money-making. Not yet did America fully realize that the war was a struggle of ideals which must concern every one closely. In such an atmosphere the idealistic policy of Wilson was not easily understood.

The President himself cannot escape a large share of the blame for America's blindness to the issue. During the first twelve months of the war, when the country looked to him for leadership, he had, purposely or otherwise, fostered the forces of pacifism and encouraged the advocates of national isolation. He had underlined the separation of the United States from everything that went on in Europe and insisted that in the issues of the war the American people had no interest. In deference to the spirit of pacifism that engrossed the Middle West, he had opposed the movement for military preparedness. When, late in 1915, Wilson changed his attitude and attempted to arouse the country to a sense of American interest in world affairs and to the need of preparing to accept responsibility, he encountered the opposition of forces which he himself had helped to vitalize.

Popular education, especially upon the Atlantic coast, was further hampered by the personal irritation which the President aroused. Disliked when inaugurated, he had attracted bitter enmity among the business men who dominate opinion in New England and the Eastern States. They accused him of truckling to labor. They were wearied by his idealism, which seemed to them all words and no deeds. They regarded his handling of foreign affairs, whether in the Mexican or submarine crises, as weak and vacillating. He was, in Rooseveltian nomenclature, a "pussyfooter." Hence grew up the tradition, which was destined to endure among many elements of opinion, that everything advocated by Wilson must, simply by reason of its authorship, be essentially wrong. The men of Boston, New York, and Philadelphia were beginning to give over their attitude of isolation and admit with Roosevelt that the United States ought to stand with the Entente. The Wilsonian doctrine of service to the world, however, was not to their taste, partly because they did not like Wilson.

It was to the rural districts of the upper Mississippi and to the South that the President looked most eagerly for support of his new policy. These were the regions where indifference to and ignorance of foreign affairs had been most conspicuous, but they were also the regions where the President's personal influence was strongest; finally they were the districts where extreme pacifism was most deeply embedded. If Wilson's championship of the rights of liberty throughout the world could be accomplished by pacific methods, they would follow him; but if it meant war, no one could guarantee what their attitude might be. Bryan was popular in those parts. As yet Wilson, while he had formulated his policy in broad terms, had not indicated the methods or mechanism by which his principles were to be put into operation. He would without question encounter strong opposition among the German-Americans; he would find the attitude of the Irish foes of the Entente hostile; he would find the Pacific coast more interested in Japanese immigration than in the ideals of the European war. Fortunately events were to unify the heterogeneous elements of the country, at least for the moment, in a way that simplified greatly the President's problem. Not the least of the unifying forces was to be found in German psychology, which led the Imperial Government to believe that the United States could be rendered helpless through the intrigues of German spies.

CHAPTER IV

PLOTS AND PREPAREDNESS

THE Government of the German Empire was inspired by a spirit that was at once modern and medieval, and this contradictory spirit manifested itself in the ways and means employed to win the sympathy of the United States and to prevent it, as a neutral power, from assisting the Entente. Germany worked on the one hand by means of open propaganda, which is the method of modern commercial advertisement translated into the political field, and on the other by secret intrigue reminiscent of the days of Louis XI. Her propaganda took the form of organized campaigns to influence opinion through speeches, pamphlets, and books, which were designed to convince the country of the justice of Germany's cause and the dangers of becoming the catspaw of the Entente. Her plans of intrigue were directed towards the use of German-Americans or German spies to assist in the return of German officers from this country, to hinder the transport of Canadian troops, to destroy communications, and to hamper the output of munitions for the Entente by strikes, incendiary fires, and explosions.

During the first weeks of the war a German press bureau was established in New York for the distribution of pro-German literature and the support of the German-American press. Its activities were chiefly directed by Dr. Bernhard Dernburg, who defended Germany from the charge of responsibility for the war and expatiated upon her efficiency and the beneficence of her culture in the same breath that he attacked the commercial greed of Great Britain, the cruel autocracy of Russia, and the imperialistic designs of Japan in the Pacific. Its pamphlets went so far as to excoriate allied methods of warfare and to level accusations of inhumanity against the Belgians. It distributed broadcast throughout the country an appeal signed by ninety-three German professors and intellectuals, and countersigned by a few notable Americans, which besought the American people not to be deceived by the "lies and calumnies" of the enemies of Germany.

This propaganda left all cold except those who

already sympathized with Germany. Indeed it reacted unfavorably against the German cause, as soon as the well-authenticated reports came of German atrocities in Belgium, of the burning of the Louvain library, and of the shelling of Rheims cathedral. The efforts of German agents then shifted, concentrating in an attack upon the United States Government for its alleged unneutral attitude in permitting the export of munitions to the Entente. In some sections of the country they were able to arouse an opinion favorable to the establishment of an embargo. In the Senate, on December 10, 1914, a bill was offered by John D. Works of California providing for the prohibition of the sale of war supplies to any belligerent nation and a similar bill was fathered in the House by Charles L. Bartlett of Georgia. These efforts were warmly supported by various associations, some of which were admittedly German-American societies, although the majority attempted to conceal their partisan feeling under such titles as *American Independence Union* and *American Neutrality League*. The latter effectively displayed its interest in America and in neutrality by tumultuous singing of *Deutschland über Alles* and *Die Wacht am Rhein*. Of sincerely pacifist organizations there were not a few, among which should not be forgotten the fantastic effort of Henry Ford in December, 1915, to end the war by sending a "Peace Ship" to Europe, designed to arouse such public opinion abroad in favor of peace that "the boys would be out of the trenches by Christmas." The ship sailed, but the expedition, which was characterized by equal amounts of honesty and foolishness, broke up shortly in dissension. For the most part pacifism and pro-Germanism went hand in hand — a tragic alliance of good and evil which was to hamper later efforts to evolve an international organization for the preservation of peace.

The attempts of German propagandists to influence the policy of the Government met, as we have seen, the stubborn resolve of the President not to favor one camp of the belligerents by a departure from international custom and law during the progress of the war. Their efforts, however, were not entirely relaxed. Appeals were made to workmen to stop the war by refusing to manufacture munitions; vigorous campaigns were conducted to discredit the Administration by creating the belief that it was discriminating in favor of the British. But more and more Germany took to secret intrigue, the strings of which were pulled by the military and naval attachés, von Papen and Boy-Ed. The German Ambassador, von Bernstorff, also took a lively interest in the plans to control public opinion and later to hamper munitions production. With his approval, German manufacturing companies were organized at Bridgeport and elsewhere to buy up the machinery and supplies essential to the production of powder, shrapnel, and surplus benzol; arrangements were made with the Bosch Magneto Company to enter into contracts with the Entente for fuses and at the last moment to refuse to complete the contract. Von Bernstorff was careful to avoid active participation in plots for the destruction of property; but his interest and complicity, together with that of Dr. Heinrich F. Albert, Financial Adviser of the German Embassy, are evidenced by the checks drawn on their joint account and paid to convicted criminals.

One of the first of the plots was the attempted blowing up of the international bridge at Vanceboro, Maine, on December 31, 1914. The materials for this explosion were collected and the fuse set by a German reservist lieutenant, Werner Horn, who admitted that he acted under the orders of von Papen. Another plan of the German agents was the destruction of the Welland Canal, which was entrusted to a brilliant and erratic adventurer, von der Goltz, who later confessed that he was under the supervision of von Papen and had secured his materials from Captain Hans Tauscher, the agent in New York of the Hamburg-American Line. This company was involved in securing false manifests for vessels that carried coal and supplies to German cruisers, thus defrauding the United States, and in obtaining false passports for German reservists and agents; it acted, in fact, as an American branch of the German Admiralty. More serious yet was an attempt of the naval attaché, Boy-Ed, to involve the United States and Mexico in a dispute by a plot to bring back Huerta. This unhappy Mexican leader was arrested on the Mexican border in June, 1915, and shortly afterwards died.

For some months the existence of such activities on the part of German agents had been suspected by the public. A series of disclosures followed. In July, 1915, Dr. Albert, while riding on a New York elevated train, was so careless as to set his portfolio on the seat for a few moments; it was speedily picked up by a fellow passenger who made a hasty exit. Soon afterwards the chief contents of the portfolio were published. They indicated the complicity of the German Embassy in different attempts to control the American press and to influence public opinion, and proved the energy of less notable agents in illegal undertakings. Towards the end of August, the Austrian Ambassador, Dr. Constantin Dumba, made use of an American correspondent, James F. J. Archibald by name, to carry dispatches to the Central Empires. He was arrested by the British authorities at Falmouth, and his effects proved Dumba's interest in plans to organize strikes in American munitions plants. "It is my impression," wrote the Austrian Ambassador, "that we can disorganize and hold up for months, if not entirely prevent, the manufacture of munitions in Bethlehem and the Middle West, which in the opinion of the German military attaché, is of great importance and amply outweighs the expenditure of money involved." Archibald also carried a letter from von Papen to his wife in which he wrote: "I always say to these idiotic Yankees that they had better hold their tongues." Its publication did not serve to allay the warmth of American feeling.

It was with great satisfaction, therefore, that the public learned in September that President Wilson had requested the recall of Ambassador Dumba in the following words: "By reason of the admitted purpose and intent of Ambassador Dumba to conspire to cripple legitimate industries of the people of the United States and to interrupt their legitimate trade, and by reason of the flagrant diplomatic impropriety in employing an American citizen protected by an American passport, as a secret bearer of official despatches through the lines of the enemy of Austria-Hungary. . . . Mr. Dumba is no longer acceptable to the Government of the United States." The two German attachés were given a longer shrift, but on the 30th of November von Bernstorff was told that they were no longer acceptable; von Papen sailed on the 22d of December and was followed a week later by Boy-Ed.

During the two preceding months there had been a constant series of strikes and explosions in munitions plants and industrial works, and public opinion was now thoroughly aroused. The feeling that Germany and Austria were thus through their agents virtually carrying on warfare in the United States was intensified by the revelations of Dr. Joseph Goričar, formerly an Austrian consul, but a Jugoslav who sympathized with the Entente; according to his statement every Austrian consul in the country was "a center of intrigue of the most criminal character." His charges came at the moment when Americans were reading that the number of strikes in munitions plants was unparalleled, no less than one hundred and two in a few months, of which fifty were in Bridgeport, which was known to be a center of German activities. Explosions and fires at the plants of the Bethlehem Steel Company and the Baldwin Locomotive Works, and at the Roebling wire-rope shop in Trenton were of mysterious origin.

To what extent explosions in munitions plants were the result of German incendiarism and not of an accidental nature, it is difficult to determine. But the Department of Justice was so thoroughly convinced of the far-reaching character of German plots that President Wilson, in his annual message of December, 1915, frankly denounced the "hyphenates" who lent their aid to such intrigues. "I am sorry to say that the gravest threats against our national peace and safety have been uttered within our own borders. There are citizens of the United States . . . who have poured the poison of disloyalty into the very arteries of our national life; who have sought to bring the authority and good name of our Government into contempt, to destroy our industries wherever they thought it effective for their vindictive purposes to strike at them, and

to debase our politics to the uses of foreign intrigue."
His attack drew forth the bitter resentment of the
foreign language press, but was hailed with delight
in the East, where German intrigues aroused as
great excitement against the Fatherland as the submarine campaign. Nor was it calmed by the continuance of fires and explosions and the evident
complicity of German officials. During the spring
of 1916 a German agent, von Igel, who occupied the
former offices of von Papen, was arrested, and the
activities of Franz von Rintelen, who had placed
incendiary bombs on vessels leaving New York
with food and supplies for the Allies, were published. Taken in conjunction with the sinking of
the *Sussex*, German plots were now stimulating
the American people to a keen sense of their interest in the war, and preparing them effectively for a
new attitude toward foreign affairs in general.

It was inevitable that such revelations should
have created a widespread demand for increased
military efficiency. The nation was approaching
the point where force might become necessary, and
yet it was in no way prepared for warfare, either on
land or sea. During the first months of the war the
helplessness of the United States had been laid bare
by General Leonard Wood, who declared that we

had never fought a really first-class nation and "were pitifully unprepared, should such a calamity be thrust upon us." The regular army "available to face such a crisis" would be "just about equal to the police forces of Boston, New York, and Philadelphia." The "preparedness movement" thus inaugurated was crystallized by the formation of the National Security League, designed to organize citizens in such a way "as may make practical an intelligent expression of public opinion and may ensure for the nation an adequate system of national defense." Pacifists and pro-Germans immediately organized in opposition; and the movement was hampered by President Wilson's unwillingness to coöperate in any way. He was flatly opposed, in the autumn of 1914 and the spring of the following year, to compulsory military service: "We will not ask our young men to spend the best years of their lives making soldiers of themselves." He insisted that the American people had always been able to defend themselves and should be able to continue to do so without altering their military traditions. It must not be forgotten that at this time Wilson still believed in absolute isolation and refused to consider force as an element in our foreign policy. His attitude was sufficient to render fruitless various

6

resolutions presented by Congressman Augustus P. Gardner and Senator George E. Chamberlain, who proposed improvements in the military system. Congress was pacifically-minded. This was the time when many Congressmen were advocating an embargo on arms, and so far from desiring to learn how to make and use munitions of war they concentrated their efforts on methods of preventing their export to the Allies.

The preparedness movement, none the less, spread through the country and the influence of the National Security League did much to inform the public. In the summer of 1915 there was organized at Plattsburg, New York, under the authority of General Wood, a civilian camp designed to give some experience in the rudiments of military science. It was not encouraged by the Administration, but at the end of the year the President himself confessed that he had been converted. He was about to abandon his policy of isolation for his new ideal of international service, and he realized the logical necessity of supporting it by at least a show of force. Mere negative "neutrality" no longer sufficed. His fear that greater military strength might lead to an aggressive spirit in the country had been obliterated by the attacks of submarines and by the German plots. He admitted frankly that he had changed his mind. "I would be ashamed," he said, "if I had not learned something in fourteen months." To the surprise of many who had counted upon his pacific tendencies to the end, he did what he had not heretofore done for any of his policies; he left his desk in Washington and took to the platform.

During January and February, 1916, President Wilson delivered a succession of speeches in Pittsburgh, Cleveland, Chicago, Milwaukee, St. Louis, and other places in the upper Mississippi Valley, emphasizing his conversion to preparedness. Aware that his transformation would be regarded as anti-German and tending to draw the United States into the conflict, he apparently sought out pro-German and pacifist centers, and for the first time utilized something of the traditional "patriotic" style to rouse those citizens who, as yet, failed to appreciate the significance of the international situation. "I know that you are depending upon me to keep the nation out of war. So far I have done so, and I pledge you my word that, God helping me, I will — if it is possible. You have laid another duty upon me. You have bidden me see that nothing stains or impairs the honor of the United States. And that is a matter not within my control. That depends upon what others do, not upon what the Government of the United States does, and therefore there may be at any moment a time when I cannot both preserve the honor and the peace of the United States. Do not exact of me an impossible and contradictory thing, but stand ready and insist that everybody that represents you should stand ready to provide the means for maintaining the honor of the United States." And later: "America cannot be an ostrich with its head in the sand. America cannot shut itself out from the rest of the world. . . . Do you want the situation to be such that all the President can do is to write messages, to utter words of protest? If these breaches of international law which are in daily danger of occurring should touch the very vital interests and honor of the United States, do you wish to do nothing about it? Do you wish to have all the world say that the flag of the United States, which we all love, can be stained with impunity?" What a transformation from those days of December, 1914, when he believed that military preparation would prove that the American people had been thrown off their balance by a war with which they had nothing to do! And what a revelation of the wounds inflicted by the barbed taunts cast against the President for his patience in the writing of diplomatic notes!

Had the President carried his enthusiasm into actual accomplishment and provided for effective military and naval preparation, his claim to the title of great statesman would be more clear. Unfortunately when it came to forcing Congress to take the necessary steps, he failed. The inertia and reluctance of pacifist or partisan representatives would have been broken by Roosevelt. But Wilson did mere lip-service to the principle of military efficiency. The bills introduced in Congress were denounced by military experts as half-measures likely to produce no efficient result, and the President, who in most matters was determined to dominate, in this permitted congressional committees to have their way. The protests of the Secretary of War, Lindley M. Garrison, led to his resignation; and (most curious development) the President replaced him by a man, Newton D. Baker, who, whatever his capacity, was generally known as a pacifist. Wilson's intelligence told him that military preparation was necessary, if his policy of international service was to be anything more than academic; but his pacific instincts prevented him from securing real military efficiency.

An example of the unreadiness of the United States was furnished in the late spring and summer of 1916, when relations with Mexico became strained almost to the breaking point. President Wilson's handling of the knotty Mexican problem had been characteristic. He had temporized in the hope that anything like a break might be avoided and was resolutely opposed to formal armed intervention. But after refusing to recognize Huerta, who had gained his position of provisional president of Mexico through the murder of Madero, in which he was evidently implicated, the President had ordered the occupation of Vera Cruz by United States troops in retaliation for the arrest of an American landing party and Huerta's refusal to fire an apologetic salute. Huerta was forced to give up his position and fled, but the crisis continued and American-Mexican relations were not improved. The country was left in the hands of three rival presidents, of whom Carranza proved the strongest, and, after an attempt at mediation in which the three chief South American powers participated, President Wilson decided to recognize him. But Mexican conditions remained chaotic and American interests in Mexico were either threatened. or destroyed. In the spring of 1916 an attack on American territory led by a bandit, Francisco Villa, again roused Wilson to action. He dispatched General John J. Pershing across the border to pursue and catch Villa. The expedition was difficult, but well-conducted; it extended far south of the frontier and provoked the protests of Carranza. At the moment when Pershing's advance guard seemed to have its hands on the bandit, orders were given to cease the pursuit.

The opponents of the Administration had some excuse for laughing at the "inglorious and ineffectual war" thus waged. It had failed to result in the capture of Villa and it gave rise to serious danger of an open break with Mexico. On the 21st of June an attack at Carrizal by Carranza's troops resulted in the capture of some United States cavalrymen and the mobilization of the national guard troops for the protection of the border. But President Wilson was not to be drawn into intervention. He might be compelled to exercise force in carrying out his ideals of international service against an international criminal like Germany; he would not use it against a weaker neighbor and particularly at the moment when the United States must be free to face European complications. But the Mexican crisis proved definitely the weakness of the military system. Though the regulars who accompanied Pershing proved their worth, the clumsy inefficient mobilization of the National Guard, on the other hand, indicated as plainly as possible the lack of trained troops and officers.

The President's determination not to intervene in Mexico probably assured him many votes in the pacifist regions of the Middle West in the presidential election of 1916. That he would be renominated by the Democrats was a foregone conclusion. He had alienated the machine leaders by his strict domination of Congress and the party; if he had permitted certain political leaders to distribute offices for necessary organization interests, he had seen to it, none the less, that the Democratic bosses had no share in the determination of policies. Still they could not hope to prevent his nomination. Whatever chance the party might have in the coming election lay in the personal strength of Wilson with the masses. In the South and the districts west of the Mississippi he was regarded as the greatest Democrat since Jackson. His patience in dealing with Germany, as with Carranza, convinced them of his desire for peace; the slogan, "He has kept us out of war," was a powerful argument in those regions. His attitude towards labor had been friendly, so that the support of the unions in the large industrial centers might be expected. Placards were posted showing a poor man's family with the caption, "He has protected me and mine," in answer to the Republican posters which showed a widow and orphans (presumably of a drowned American citizen) and the caption, "He has neglected me and mine." The remnants of the Progressives, who were not purely Roosevelt supporters, were attracted by Wilson's legislative programme and record of accomplishment. He could look to an independent vote such as no other Democrat could hope for.

Despite this strength, the Republican leaders, if they could succeed in effecting a reunion of their party, awaited the results of the election with confidence. They counted chiefly upon the personal unpopularity of Wilson on the Atlantic seaboard and the normal Republican vote in the industrial centers of the Middle West. His foreign policy, east of the Mississippi, was generally looked upon as anæmic and nebulous. He had permitted, so the Republicans contended, the honor of the country to be stained and Americans to be destroyed, without effective action. His early opposition to preparedness and the half-hearted measures of army reform had proved his weakness, at least to the satisfaction of Republican stump orators. He had won the hearty dislike of the bankers, the manufacturers, and the merchants by his attacks on capitalist interests and by his support of labor unions. The Clayton Act, which exempted strikes from Federal injunctions, and the Adamson Act, which granted, under threat, the immediate demands of the striking railroad employees, were cited as clear proof of his demagogic character. Furthermore, while he alienated the pro-Entente elements in New England and the Eastern States, he had drawn upon himself the hatred of the German-Americans by his attacks upon hyphenates and his refusal to accept an embargo on American munitions.

Had the Republicans been willing to accept Theodore Roosevelt, victory would probably have come to them. He alone could have gathered in the Progressive and independent vote, and that of the Pacific coast, which ultimately went to Wilson. But the Old Guard of the Republicans refused to consider Roosevelt; they could not take a man who had broken party lines four years before; above all they wanted a "safe and sane" President, who would play the political game according to rule — the rule of the bosses — and they knew that were Roosevelt elected they could not hope to share in the spoils. The Republican convention ultimately settled upon Charles E. Hughes, who certainly was not beloved by the bosses, but who was regarded as "steadier" than Roosevelt. The latter, in order to defeat Wilson, refused the offer of the Progressives, practically disbanded the party he had created, and called upon his friends to return with him to their first allegiance.

Hughes did not prove a strong candidate. Whereas Wilson had stated his position on the German-American problem plainly, "I neither seek the favor nor fear the displeasure of that small alien element among us which puts loyalty to any foreign power before loyalty to the United States," Hughes was ordered by his party managers not to offend foreign-born voters, and in his attempt to steer a middle course, gave a clear impression of vacillation. Many of those who had been most thoroughly disgusted with Wilson turned back to him again, as the weeks passed and Hughes more and more sought refuge in vague generalizations. In a campaign in which the issues were largely personal

the Republican candidate's failure to evolve a constructive policy greatly weakened him, especially
as Wilson had the advantage of the maxim that it
is best not to change horses in the middle of the
stream. Finally, Hughes did not prove adept in
reconciling the Progressives. Indeed it was said to
be a political *gaucherie* on his part, or that of his
advisers, which alienated the friends of Governor Hiram Johnson of California and threw the
electoral vote of that State to Wilson.

California turned the scale. When on the evening of the 7th of November the first returns came in
and it was seen that Wilson had lost New York and
Illinois, the election of Hughes was generally conceded. Even the *New York Times* and the *World*
admitted Wilson's defeat. But the next morning,
news from the west indicated that the President
still had a chance. Later in the day the chance
grew larger; he had won Ohio; Minnesota and California were doubtful. In both States voting was
close; if Wilson won either the election would be
his. It was not until the 11th of November that
the returns from California definitely showed a
small Wilson plurality, and only on the 21st that
the Republicans finally abandoned hope. Wilson
had secured 277 electoral votes to 254 for Hughes.

He had been saved by the pacifist Middle and Far West, in combination with the South. But the victory meant something far different from peace at any price.

CHAPTER V

AMERICA DECIDES

THE presidential campaign of 1916, taken in conjunction with the increasing tension of European
relations, forced Wilson to a further development
of his international ideals and a more definite
formulation of the means by which to attain them.
As we have observed, the spring of that year saw
him reject the doctrine of isolation. "We are participants," he said on the 27th of May, "whether
we would or not, in the life of the world. The interests of all nations are our own also. We are partners with the rest. What affects mankind is inevitably our affair as well as the affair of the nations of
Europe and of Asia." This recognition of our interest in world affairs immediately took him con-
siderably beyond the position he had assumed
during the earlier stages of the submarine controversy. Until the spring of 1916 he had restricted
his aims to the championship of neutral and human

rights in time of war. But now he began to demand something more far-reaching, namely a system that would prevent unjust war altogether and would protect the rights of all peoples in time of peace. He insisted, in this same speech of the 27th of May, before the League to Enforce Peace at Washington, "First that every people has a right to choose the sovereignty under which they shall live. . . . Second, that the small states of the world have a right to enjoy the same respect for their sovereignty and for their territorial integrity that great and powerful nations expect and insist upon. And, third, that the world has a right to be free from every disturbance of its peace that has its origin in aggression and disregard of the rights of peoples and nations." These words sum up the gist of his international aims during the three following years. His later speeches are merely refinement of details.

In order that these ends might be secured it was necessary that some international system be inaugurated other than that which had permitted the selfishness of the great powers to produce war in the past. In his search for a concrete mechanism to realize his ideals and secure them from violation, Wilson seized upon the essential principles of the

League to Enforce Peace, of which William Howard Taft was president. The basis of permanent peace, Wilson insisted, could be found only by substituting international coöperation in place of conflict, through a mobilization of the public opinion of the world against international lawbreakers: "an universal association of the nations to maintain the inviolate security of the highway of the seas for the common and unhindered use of all the nations of the world, and to prevent any war begun either contrary to treaty covenants or without warning and full submission of the causes to the opinion of the world — a virtual guarantee of territorial integrity and political independence." These were the principles and methods which formed the keynote of his foreign policy until the end of the Peace Conference. The first part of the programme, that which concerned the security of the seas and which originated in the particular circumstances of 1915, faded from his sight to a large extent; the second portion, more general in its nature, became of increasing importance until, as Article X of the League Covenant, it seemed to him the heart of the entire settlement.

The unselfish nature of his idealism, as well as his continued detachment from both camps of the belligerents, was obvious. "We have nothing material of any kind to ask for ourselves," he said, "and are quite aware that we are in no sense or degree parties to the present quarrel. Our interest is only in peace and in its future guarantees." But *noblesse oblige*, and we must serve those who have not had our good fortune. "The commands of democracy are as imperative as its privileges are wide and generous. Its compulsion is upon us. . . . We are not worthy to stand here unless we ourselves be in deed and truth real democrats and servants of mankind."

That the United States might be drawn into the conflict evidently seemed possible to the President, despite pacific whispers that came from Germany in the spring and summer of 1916. There was a note of apprehension in his speeches. No one could tell when the extremist faction in Berlin might gain control and withdraw the *Sussex* pledge. The temper of Americans was being tried by continued sinkings, although the exact circumstances of each case were difficult to determine. The attacks made by the German U-53 immediately off the American coast and the deportation of Belgian civilians into Germany made more difficult the preservation of amicable relations. In view of the possibility of war

7

Wilson wanted to define the issue exactly. "We have never yet," he said at Omaha, a peace center, on the 5th of October, "sufficiently formulated our programme for America with regard to the part she is going to play in the world, and it is imperative that she should formulate it at once. . . . It is very important that the statesmen of other parts of the world should understand America. . . . We are holding off, not because we do not feel concerned, but because when we exert the force of this nation we want to know what we are exerting it for." Ten days later at Shadowlawn he said: "Define the elements, let us know that we are not fighting for the prevalence of this nation over that, for the ambitions of this group of nations as compared with the ambitions of that group of nations; let us once be convinced that we are called in to a great combination to fight for the rights of mankind and America will unite her force and spill her blood for the great things which she has always believed in and followed." He thus gave warning that the United States might have to fight. He wanted to be certain, however, that it did not fight as so many other nations have fought, greedily or vindictively, but rather as in a crusade and for clearly defined ideals.

His reëlection gave to the President an opportunity for bringing before the world his international aims. He purposed not merely to end the existing conflict but also to provide a basis for permanent peace and the security of democracy. During the early summer of 1916 he had received from Berlin hints that his mediation would not be unacceptable and it is possible that he planned at that time new efforts to bring the war to a close. But such a step was bound to be regarded as pro-German and in the state of opinion immediately after the *Sussex* crisis would have produced a storm of American protests. Then the entrance of Rumania into the war so encouraged the Entente powers that there seemed little chance of winning French and British acceptance of mediation. The presidential election further delayed any overt step towards peace negotiations. Finally the wave of anti-German feeling that swept the United States in November, on account of Belgian deportations, induced Wilson to hold back the note which he had already drafted. But it was important not to delay his pacific efforts over-long, since news came to Washington that unless Germany could obtain a speedy peace the extremist group in Berlin would insist upon a resumption of "ruthless" submarine warfare. In these circumstances, early in December, the President prepared to issue his note.

But Germany acted more rapidly. Warned of Wilson's purpose the Berlin Government, on December 12, 1916, proposed negotiations. The occasion seemed to them propitious. Rumania had gone down to disastrous defeat. Russia was torn by corruption and popular discontent. On the western front, if the Germans had failed at Verdun, they were aware of the deep disappointment of the Allies at the paltry results of the great Somme drive. German morale at home was weakening; but if the Allies could be pictured as refusing all terms and determined upon the destruction of Germany, the people would doubtless agree to the unrestricted use of the submarine as purely defensive in character, even if it brought to the Allies the questionable assistance of America. The German note itself contained no definite terms. But its boastful tone permitted the interpretation that Germany would consider no peace which did not leave Central and Southeastern Europe under Teuton domination; the specific terms later communicated to the American Government in secret, verified this suspicion. A thinly veiled threat to neutral nations was to be read between the lines of the German suggestion of negotiations.

Although it was obvious that he would be accused of acting in collusion with Germany, President Wilson decided not to postpone the peace note already planned. He looked upon the crisis as serious, for if peace were not secured at this time the chances of the United States remaining out of the war were constantly growing less. If he could compel a clear definition of war aims on both sides, the mutual suspicion of the warring peoples might be removed; the German people might perceive that the war was not in reality for them one of defense; or finally the Allies, toward whom Wilson was being driven by the threats of German extremists, might define their position in such terms as would justify him before the world in joining with them in a conflict not waged for selfish national purposes but for the welfare of humanity. Issued on December 18, 1916, his note summed up the chief points of his recently developed policy. It emphasized the interest of the United States in the future peace of the world, the irreparable injury to civilization that might result from a further continuance of the existing struggle, the advantages that would follow an explicit exposure of belligerent purposes, and the possibility of making "the permanent concord of the nations a hope of the immediate future, a concert of nations immediately practicable."

As a step towards peace the note was unsuccessful. Germany was evasive. There was nothing her Government wanted less than the definite exposure of her purposes that Wilson asked. Her leaders were anxious to begin negotiations while German armies still held conquered territories as pawns to be used at the peace table. They would not discuss a League of Nations until Germany's continental position was secured. The Allies on the other hand would not make peace with an unbeaten Germany, which evidently persisted in the hope of dominating weaker nationalities and said no word of reparations for the acknowledged wrongs committed. Feeling ran high in England and France because Wilson's note had seemed to place the belligerents on the same moral plane, in its statement that the objects on both sides "are virtually the same, as stated in general terms to their own people and to the world." The statement was verbally accurate and rang with a certain grim irony which may have touched Wilson's sense of humor. But the Allies were not in a state of mind to appreciate such humor. Their official answer, however, was frank, and in substance accepted the principles of permanent peace propounded by Wilson. It was evident to most Americans that the main purpose of Germany was to establish herself as the dominating power of the continent and possibly of the world; the aim of the Allies, on the other hand, seemed to be the peace of the world based upon democracy and justice rather than material force.

The President's attempt thus cleared the air. It made plain to the majority of Americans that in sympathy, at least, the United States must be definitely aligned with Great Britain and France. Furthermore the replies of the belligerents gave to Wilson an opportunity to inform the world more definitely of the aims of the United States, in case it should be drawn into the war. This he did in a speech delivered to the Senate on January 22, 1917. America would play her part in world affairs, he said, but the other nations must clearly understand the conditions of our participation. The basis of peace must be the right of each individual nation to decide its destiny for itself without interference from a stronger alien power. "I am proposing as it were, that the nations should with one accord adopt the doctrine of President Monroe as the doctrine of the world: that no nation should seek to extend its polity over any other nation or people, but that every people should be left free to determine its own polity, its own way of development, unhindered, unthreatened, unafraid, the little along with the great and powerful." Instead of the old system of alliances there should be a general concert of powers: "There is no entangling alliance in a concert of powers. When all unite to act in the same sense and with the same purpose, all act in the common interest and are free to live their own lives under a common protection." As the result of such a concert no one power would dominate the sea or the land; armaments might safely be limited; peace would be organized by the major force of mankind. As a guarantee of future justice and tranquillity the terms that settled the present war must be based upon justice and not be of the sort ordinarily dictated by the victor to the vanquished. It must be a "peace without victory." Thus while Wilson warned Germany that her ambitions for continental domination would not be tolerated, he also warned the Allies that they could not count upon the United States to help them to crush Germany for their selfish individual purposes.

This speech, despite the unfortunate phrase

"peace without victory," was hailed in all liberal circles, amongst the Allies and in the United States, as a noble charter of the new international order. Wilson had expressed the hope that he was "speaking for the silent mass of mankind everywhere who have as yet had no place or opportunity to speak their real hearts out concerning the death and ruin they see to have come already upon the persons and the homes they hold most dear." This hope was doubtless realized. The first reaction in France and England was one of rather puzzled contempt, if we may judge by the press. But the newspaper writers soon found that what Wilson said many people had been thinking, and waiting for some one to say. Hall Caine wrote to the *Public Ledger*, "Let President Wilson take heart from the first reception of his remarkable speech. The best opinion here is one of deep feeling and profound admiration." From that moment Wilson began to approach the position he was shortly to hold—that of moral leader of the world.

The President had been anxious to make plain his principles, before the United States became involved in the conflict through the withdrawal of German submarine pledges, as well as to convince the world that every honest effort possible had been made to preserve the peace. He was only just in time. Already the advocates of ruthlessness in Berlin had persuaded the Kaiser and Bethmann-Hollweg. They recognized that the resumption of unrestricted submarine warfare meant, in all probability, the intervention of the United States, but they recked little of the consequences. On January 16, 1917, the Kaiser telegraphed: "If a break with America is unavoidable, it cannot be helped; we proceed." The same day the Secretary of Foreign Affairs, Zimmermann, telegraphed to the German Minister in Mexico, instructing him to form an alliance with Mexico in the event of war between Germany and the United States, and to offer as bribe the States of New Mexico, Arizona, and Texas; he also suggested the possibility of winning Japan from her allegiance to the Entente and persuading her to enter this prospective alliance.

On the 31st of January, von Bernstorff threw off the mask. The German Ambassador informed our Government of the withdrawal of the *Sussex* pledge. On and after the 1st of February, German submarines would sink on sight all ships met within a delimited zone around the British Isles and in the Mediterranean. They would permit the sailing of a few American steamships, however, provided they followed a certain defined route to Falmouth and nowhere else, and provided there were marked "on ship's hull and superstructure three vertical stripes one meter wide, to be painted alternately white and red. Each mast should show a large flag checkered white and red, and the stern the American national flag. Care should be taken that during dark, national flag and painted marks are easily recognizable from a distance, and that the boats are well lighted throughout." Other conditions followed. There might sail one steamship a week "in each direction, with arrival at Falmouth on Sunday and departure from Falmouth on Wednesday." Furthermore the United States Government must guarantee "that no contraband (according to the German contraband list) is carried by those steamships." Such were the orders issued to the United States. No native American could escape the humor of the stipulations, which for a moment prevented the national irritation from swelling into an outburst of deep-seated wrath.

There seems to have been little hesitation on the part of the President. On April 19, 1916, he had warned Germany that unrestricted submarine warfare meant a severance of diplomatic relations. Now, on February 3, 1917, addressing both houses cf Congress, he announced that those relations had been broken. Von Bernstorff was given his papers and the American Ambassador, James W. Gerard, was recalled from Berlin. No other course of action could have been contemplated in view of the formality of the President's warning and the definiteness of Germany's defiance. Despite the protests of scattered pacifists, the country was as nearly a unit in its approval of Wilson's action as its heterogeneous national character permitted. All the pent-up emotions of the past two years found expression in quiet but unmistakable applause at the departure of the German Ambassador.

The promptitude of the President's dismissal of von Bernstorff did not conceal the disappointment which he experienced from Germany's revelation of her true purposes. He seems to have hoped to the end that the German liberals would succeed in bringing their Government to accept moderate terms of peace. Even now he expressed the hope that Germany's actions would not be such as to force the United States into the War: "I refuse to believe that it is the intention of the German authorities to do in fact what they have warned us they will feel at liberty to do. . . . Only actual overt acts on their part can make me believe it even now."

But "if American ships and American lives should in fact be sacrificed by their naval commanders in heedless contravention of the just and reasonable understandings of international law and the obvious dictates of humanity, I shall take the liberty of coming again before the Congress to ask that authority be given me to use any means that may be necessary for the protection of our seamen and our people in the prosecution of their peaceful and legitimate errands on the high seas. I can do nothing less. I take it for granted that all neutral governments will take the same course." He was careful, moreover, to underline the fact that his action was dictated always by a consistent desire for peace: "We wish to serve no selfish ends. We seek merely to stand true alike in thought and in action to the immemorial principles of our people. . . . These are the bases of peace, not war. God grant we may not be challenged to defend them by acts of willful injustice on the part of the Government of Germany!"

But Germany proceeded heedlessly. Warned that American intervention would result only from overt acts, the German Admiralty hastened to commit such acts. From the 3d of February to the 1st of April, eight American vessels were sunk by submarines and forty-eight American lives thus lost. Because of the practical blockade of American ports which followed the hesitation of American shipping interests to send boats unarmed into the dangers of the "war zone," President Wilson came again to Congress on the 26th of February to ask authority to arm merchant vessels for purposes of defense. Again he stressed his unwillingness to enter upon formal warfare and emphasized the idealistic aspect of the issue: "It is not of material interests merely that we are thinking. It is, rather, of fundamental human rights, chief of all the right of life itself. I am thinking not only of the rights of Americans to go and come about their proper business by way of the sea, but also of something much deeper, much more fundamental than that. I am thinking of those rights of humanity without which there is no civilization. . . . I cannot imagine any man with American principles at his heart hesitating to defend these things."

Blinded by prejudice and tradition, a handful of Senators, twelve "willful men," as Wilson described them, blocked, through a filibuster, the resolution granting the power requested by the President. But the storm of popular obloquy which covered them proved that the nation as a whole was determined to support him in the defense of American rights. The country was stirred to the depths. The publication of the plans of Germany for involving the United States in war with Mexico and Japan came merely as added stimulus. So also of the story of the cruelties heaped by the Germans on the American prisoners of the *Yarrowdale*. There was so much of justice in the cause that passion was notable by its absence. When finally on the 17th of March news came of the torpedoing of the *Vigilancia* without warning, America was prepared and calmly eager for the President's demand that Congress recognize the existence of a state of war.

The demand was made by Wilson in an extraordinary joint session of Congress, held on the 2d of April. In this, possibly his greatest speech, he was careful not to blur the idealistic principles which, since the spring of 1916, he had been formulating. War existed because Germany by its actions had thrust upon the United States the status of belligerent. But the American people must meet the challenge with their purpose clearly before them. "We must put excited feeling away. Our motive will not be revenge or the victorious assertion of the physical might of the nation, but only the vindication of right, of human right, of which we are only a single champion. . . . The wrongs against which we now array ourselves are no common wrongs; they cut to the very roots of human life." He went on to define the objects of the war more specifically, referring to his earlier addresses: "Our object now, as then, is to vindicate the principles of peace and justice in the life of the world as against selfish and autocratic power and to set up amongst the really free and self-governed peoples of the world such a concert of purpose and action as will henceforth ensure the observance of those principles." Democracy must be the soul of the new international order: "A steadfast concert for peace can never be maintained except by a partnership of democratic nations. No autocratic government could be trusted to keep faith within it or observe its covenants. . . . Only free peoples can hold their purpose and their honor steady to a common end and prefer the interests of mankind to any narrow interest of their own." Because the existing German Government was clearly at odds with all such ideals, "We are glad, now that we see the facts with no veil of false pretense about them, to fight thus for the ultimate peace of the world and for the liberation of its peoples, the German people included: for the rights

of nations great and small and the privilege of men
everywhere to choose their way of life and of obedi-
ence. The world must be made safe for democracy. Its peace must be planted upon the tested
foundations of political liberty."

Wilson thus imagined the war as a crusade, the
sort of crusade for American ideals which Clay and
Webster once imagined. He was in truth originat-
ing nothing, but rather resuscitating the generous
dreams which had once inspired those statesmen.
In conclusion, he reiterated his love of peace.
"But the right is more precious than peace, and we
shall fight for the things which we have always carried nearest our hearts, — for democracy, for the
right of those who submit to authority to have a
voice in their own governments, for the rights and
liberties of small nations, for a universal dominion
of right by such a concert of free peoples as shall
bring peace and safety to all nations and make the
world itself at last free." At the moment of the
declaration of war Wilson was still the man of peace,
and the war upon which the nation was embarking
was, in his mind, a war to ensure peace. To such a
task of peace and liberation, he concluded in a pero-
ration reminiscent of Lincoln and Luther, "we can
dedicate our lives and our fortunes, everything that

8

we are and everything that we have, with the pride of those who know that the day has come when America is privileged to spend her blood and her might for the principles that gave her birth and happiness and the peace which she has treasured. God helping her, she can do no other."

How many Americans caught the real significance of Wilson's thought with all its consequences is doubtful. The country certainly looked upon the war as a crusade. But there was in the national emotion much that did not accord with the ideals of Wilson. The people hated Germany for the sinking of the *Lusitania* and all the other submarine outrages, for her crimes in Belgium, for the plots and explosions in this country, for the Zimmermann note, and finally for her direct and insulting defiance of American rights. They recognized that the Allies were fighting for civilization; they sympathized with the democracies of Europe, of which, since the Russian revolution of March, the Allied camp was composed, and they wanted to help them. They feared for America's safety in the future, if Germany won the war. Most Americans entered the struggle, therefore, with a sober gladness, based partly on emotional, partly on quixotic, and partly on selfish grounds. But nearly all fought rather to beat Germany than to secure a new international order.) Hence it was that after Germany was beaten, Wilson was destined to discover that his idealistic preaching had not fully penetrated, and that he had failed to educate his country, as completely as he believed, to the ideal of a partnership of democratic and peace-loving peoples as the essential condition of a new and safe world.

CHAPTER VI

THE NATION IN ARMS

When Congress declared that the United States was in a state of war with Germany, on April 6, 1917, the public opinion of the country was unified to a far greater extent than at the beginning of any previous war. The extreme patience displayed by President Wilson had its reward. When the year opened the majority of citizens doubtless still hoped that peace was possible. But German actions in February and March had gone far towards the education of the popular mind, and the final speeches of the President crystallized conviction. By April there were few Americans, except those in whom pacifism was a mania, who were not convinced that war with Germany was the only course consistent with either honor or safety. It is probable that many did not understand exactly the ideals that actuated Wilson, but nine persons out of ten believed it absolutely necessary to fight.

But, however firmly united, the country was completely unprepared for war in a military sense, and must now pay the penalty for President Wilson's opposition to adequate improvement of the military system in 1915 and for the half-hearted measures taken in 1916. Total military forces, including regular army, national guard, and reserves amounted to hardly three hundred thousand men and less than ten thousand officers. Even the regular army was by no means ready for immediate participation in the sort of fighting demanded by the European war; and, even if adequate troops were raised, the lack of trained officers would create the most serious difficulties. No wonder that the German General Staff ranked the United States, from the military point of view, somewhere between Belgium and Portugal. Furthermore, military experts had been discouraged by the attitude of the Administration. The Secretary of War, Newton D. Baker, had failed, either through lack of administrative capacity or because of pacifistic tendencies, to prepare his department adequately. He had done nothing to rouse Congress or the nation from its attitude of indifference towards preparation. By faith a pacifist, he had been opposed to universal military service. An extreme liberal, he distrusted the professional military type and was to find it difficult to coöperate with the captains of industry whose assistance was essential.

Thus with a President and War Secretary, both of whom had been instinctively opposed to a large army and who had expressed their fear of the development of a militaristic spirit, and with a majority in Congress favoring the traditional volunteer system, adherence to which had cost the British thousands of lives that might better have been used at home, the building of an effective army seemed a matter of extreme doubt. Great credit must go to both President Wilson and Secretary Baker for sinking their natural instincts and seeking, as well as following, the advice of the military experts, who alone were capable of meeting the problems that arose from a war for which the nation was not prepared.

The President must face not only the special problems caused by unreadiness, but also the general difficulties which confront every American war-President and which had tried nearly to the breaking-point even the capacity of Lincoln. The President of the United States in time of war is given the supreme unified command of the army and navy.

But while the responsibility is his, actual control often rests in the hands of others. Members of Congress always take a keen interest in army matters; many of them have been or are militiamen. They have always opposed a single army which could be recruited, trained, and operated as a unit, and approved the system of State militia which makes for decentralization and gives to the separate States large influence in the formation of military policy. Even the President's control of the Federal army, regulars and volunteers, is limited by the decentralized organization of the different army bureaus, which depend upon Congress for their appropriations and which operate as almost independent and frequently competing units. The creation of a single programme for the army as a whole is thus a task of extreme difficulty.

President Wilson, as historian, was well aware of the tremendous price that had been paid in past wars for such decentralization, accompanied as it was, inevitably, by delays, misunderstandings, and mistakes. He was determined to create a single coördinating command, and his war policies were governed from beginning to end by this purpose. He set up no new machinery, but utilized as his main instrument the General Staff, which had been created in 1903 as a result of the blunders and confusion that had been so painfully manifest in the Spanish War. When the United States entered the World War the General Staff had by no means acquired the importance expected by those who had created it.[1] But to it the President turned, and it was this body enlarged in size and influence that ultimately put into operation Wilson's policy of centralization. It was in accordance with the advice of the men who composed the General Staff that the President elaborated the larger lines of the military programme, and they were the men who supervised the operation of details.

None of the processes which marked the transition of the United States from a peace to a war basis are comprehensible unless we remember that the President was constantly working to overcome the forces of decentralization, and also that the military programme was always on an emergency basis, shifting almost from week to week in accordance with developments in Europe.

[1] In April, 1917, the General Staff consisted of fifty-one officers, only nineteen of whom were on duty in Washington. Of these, eight were occupied with routine business, leaving but eleven free for the real purpose for which the staff had been created — "the study of military problems, the preparation of plans for national defense, and utilization of the military forces in time of war."

The original programme did not provide for an expeditionary force in France. During the early days of participation in the war it was generally believed that the chief contributions of the United States to Allied victory would not be directly upon the fighting front. If the United States concentrated its efforts upon financing the Allies, furnishing them with food, shipping, and the munitions which had been promised—so many persons argued—it would be doing far better than if it weakened assistance of that sort by attempting to set up and maintain a large fighting force of its own. The impression was unfortunately prevalent in civilian circles that Germany was on her last legs, and that the outcome of the war would be favorably settled before the United States could put an effective army in the field. Military experts, on the other hand, more thoroughly convinced of German strength, believed that the final campaigns could not come before the summer of 1919, and did not expect to provide a great expeditionary force previous to the spring of that year if indeed it were ever sent. Thus from opposite points of view the amateur and the professional deprecated haste in dispatching an army to France. From the moment the United States entered the war, President

Wilson certainly seems to have resolved upon the preparation of an effective fighting force, if we may judge from his insistence upon the selective draft, although he did not expect that it would be used abroad. But it may be asked whether he did not hope for the arrangement of a negotiated peace, which if not "without victory" would at least leave Germany uncrushed. It is probable that he did not yet perceive that "force to the utmost" would be necessary before peace could be secured; that realization was to come only in the dark days of 1918.

A few weeks after America's declaration of war, however, France and Great Britain dispatched missions led by Balfour, Viviani, and Joffre, to request earnestly that at least a small American force be sent overseas at once for the moral effect upon dispirited France. The plea determined the President to send General Pershing immediately with a force of about two thousand, who were followed in June and July, 1917, by sufficient additional forces to make up a division. Wilson had been authorized by Congress, under the Selective Service Act, to send four volunteer divisions abroad under the command of Roosevelt. But he refused to interfere with the plans of the military experts, who strongly objected to any volunteer forces whatever. Neither the valiant ex-President nor the prospective volunteers were trained for the warfare of the moment, and their presence in France would bring no practical good to the Allied cause; moreover the officers whom Roosevelt requested were sorely needed in American training camps.

General Pershing, to whom was now entrusted the military fortunes of the American army abroad, was an officer fifty-seven years old, who had undergone wide military and administrative experience in Cuba and the Philippines; he had been given extraordinary promotion by President Roosevelt, who had jumped him from the rank of captain to that of Brigadier General; and he had been selected to lead the punitive force dispatched in pursuit of Villa in the spring of 1916. Distinguished in appearance, with superb carriage, thin lips, and squarely-chiselled chin, he possessed military gifts of a sound rather than brilliant character. A strict disciplinarian, he failed to win from his troops that affection which the *poilus* gave to Pétain, while he never displayed the genius that compelled universal admiration for Foch. Neither ultimate success nor the stories of his dramatic remarks (as at the grave of La Fayette: "La Fayette, we are here!")

succeeded in investing him with the heroic halo that ought to come to a victorious commander. As time passes, however, Pershing takes higher rank. His insistence upon soldierly qualities, his unyielding determination to create American armies under an independent command, his skill in building up a great organization, his successful operations at St. Mihiel and in the Meuse-Argonne drive, despite faulty staff work — all these facts become more plain as we acquire perspective. If historians refuse to recognize him as a great general, they will surely describe his talents as more than adequate to the exigencies of the military situation.

The sending of the Pershing expedition did not at once alter fundamentally the original programme for raising an army of about a million men to be kept in the United States, as a reserve in case of emergency. There was no intention of sending to France more troops than would be needed to keep filled the ranks of the small expeditionary force. But the urgent representations of the Allies and reports from American officers induced a radical change in policy. The latter emphasized the unsound military position of our Allies and insisted that the deadlock could be broken and the war won only by putting a really effective American army beside the

French and British by the summer of 1918. A programme was drawn up in France and sent to the War Department, according to which an army of thirty divisions should be sent abroad before the end of that year. Throughout 1917 this plan remained rather a hope than a definite programme and it was not until early in 1918 that it was officially approved. It was thus of an emergency character and this fact combined with the indefiniteness prevalent during the autumn of 1917 to produce extreme confusion. In July, 1918, an eighty-division programme was adopted and more confusion resulted. Furthermore the entire problem was complicated by the question as to whether or not ships could be found for transportation. It had been assumed that it would take six months to transport five hundred thousand troops. But in May, 1918, and thereafter nearly three hundred thousand troops a month were carried to France, largely through tonnage obtained from the British. Such a development of transportation facilities was not and could not be foreseen. It increased the confusion. In the face of such difficulties, the problems of man-power, training, and supplies had to be met and ultimately solved, largely through the centralization carried into effect by the General Staff.

The problem of man-power had been carefully considered during the weeks that preceded our entrance into the war and the declaration of war found the Government prepared with a plan for a selective draft. On the 7th of April, the day after the declaration of war, President Wilson insisted that "the safety of the nation depended upon the measure." *selected draft.*

Congress, however, was slow to accept the principle of conscription, and the President encountered fierce opposition on the part of the advocates of the volunteer system, who were led by men of such influence as Speaker Champ Clark, House Leader Claude Kitchin, and the chairman of the House Committee on Military Affairs, Stanley H. Dent. The President was inflexible, declaring that the Administration would not "yield an inch of any essential parts of the programme for raising an army by conscription," and exercised his personal influence to its fullest extent in order to secure a favorable vote. He was ably seconded by Julius Kahn, the ranking Republican member of the House Military Committee, who was himself born in Germany. The failure of House and Senate to agree on the matter of age liability delayed action for some weeks. Finally, on May 18, 1917, what is popularly known as the Selective Service Act became law.

This Act gave to the President power to raise the regular army by enlistment to 287,000 men, to take into the Federal service all members of the national guard, and to raise by selective draft, in two installments, a force of a million troops. All men between the ages of twenty-one and thirty, both inclusive, were registered on the 5th of June; this with the subsequent registration of men coming of age later, produced an available body of more than ten millions. And when in the following year, the draft age was extended to include all men between the ages of eighteen and forty-five, both inclusive, thirteen millions more were added. From this body the names of those who were to serve were drawn by lot. All men registered were carefully classified, in order that the first chosen might be those not merely best fitted for fighting, but those whose absence on the firing line would least disturb the essential economic life of the nation. Liberal exemptions were accorded, including artisans employed in industries necessary to war production and men upon whom others were dependent. On the 20th of July the first drawings were made, and by the end of the year about half a million of the drafted men, now called the National Army, were mustered in. In the meantime enlistments in the regular army and the national guard had raised the total number of troops to about a million and a quarter and of officers to more than one hundred thousand. Less than a year later, when the armistice was signed, the army included over three and a half millions, of whom nearly two millions were in France.

The real military contribution of the United States to allied victory lay in man-power. It could not of its own resources transport the troops nor equip them completely, but the raising of an enormous number of fresh forces, partially trained, it is true, but of excellent fighting caliber, made possible the maneuvers of Foch that brought disaster to German arms. When once these armies arrived in numbers on the battle-line in France, the realization of the inexhaustible man-power of America did more than anything else to revive the spirit of the Allies and discourage the enemy.

Infinitely more difficult than the problem of man-power were those of training and supplies. As we have seen, these problems were complicated by the decision to send abroad an effective fighting force, a decision which completely changed the entire military situation. The original plan of maintaining an army only in the United States, as a reserve, permitted the questions of camps, supplies, equipment, munitions, and training to be undertaken at comparative leisure. But if a large army was to be placed in France by 1918, these problems must be solved immediately and upon an emergency basis. Hence resulted the confusion and expense which nearly led to the breakdown of the whole programme in the winter of 1917–18. The War Department faced a dilemma. If it waited until supplies were ready, the period of training would be too short. On the other hand, if it threw the new draft armies immediately into the camps, assuming that the camps could be prepared, the troops would lack the wool uniforms and blankets necessary for protection, as well as the equipment with which to drill. The second alternative appeared the less dangerous, and in September the first draft calls were made and by December the camps were filled.[1]

[1] The size of the army raised in 1917 demanded the building of enormous cantonments. Within three months of the first drawings sixteen complete cities of barracks had sprung up, each to accommodate 40,000 inhabitants. They had their officers' quarters, hospitals, sewage systems, filter plants, and garbage incinerators, electric lighting plants, libraries, theaters. By the 4th of September the National Army cantonments were ready for

9

Many apprehensions were fulfilled in fact, when the terrible winter weather came, the worst in years. The northern camps faced it with insufficient clothing. Pneumonia made its invasion. Artillerymen were trained with wooden guns; infantrymen with wooden rifles or antiquated Krags. But all the time the essential training proceeded and the calls for replacements sent by General Pershing in France were met.

The first and vital need was for officers to train the willing but inexperienced recruits. To meet this need a series of officers' training camps had been established in the spring of 1917 and continued for a year. Each camp lasted for three months, where during twelve hours a day the candidates for commissions, chiefly college graduates

---

430,000 men, two-thirds of the first draft. A single camp involved the expenditure of approximately $11,000,000. Camp Grant, at Rockford, Illinois, included 1600 buildings with space for 45,000 men and 12,000 horses. The water, which before use was tested and filtered, was supplied from six huge wells drilled 175 feet deep, carried through 38 miles of water main, and stored in reservoir tanks holding 550,000 gallons. For lighting purposes there were 1450 miles of electric wire, 1200 poles, 35,000 incandescent lamps. During the period of construction, 50 carloads of building material were daily unloaded, and for several weeks an average of 500,000 board feet of lumber set up daily. The entire construction of the camp demanded 50,000,000 feet of lumber, 700 tons of nails, 4,000,000 feet of roofing, and 3,000,000 square feet of wall board.

and young business men, were put through the most intensive drill and withering study. All told, more than eighty thousand commissions were granted through the camps, and the story of the battlefields proved at once the caliber of these amateur officers and the effectiveness of their training. Special camps, such as the school of fire at Fort Sill, carried the officers a step further, and when they went overseas they received in schools in France instruction in the latest experience of the Allied armies. The colleges of the country were also formed into training schools and ultimately about 170,000 young men, under military age, in five hundred institutions of learning, joined the Students' Army Training Corps.

In all the army schools French and British officers coöperated as instructors and gave the value of their three years' experience on the fighting front. But the traditions of the American regular army, formulated in the Indian and frontier fights, rather than the siege methods of the trenches, formed the basic principles of the instruction; General Pershing was insistent that an offensive spirit must be instilled into the new troops, a policy which received the enthusiastic endorsement of the President. The development of "a self-reliant infantry by thorough drill in the use of a rifle and in the tactics of open warfare" was always uppermost in the mind of the commander of the expeditionary force, who from first to last refused to approve the extreme specialization in trench warfare that was advised by the British and the French.

The emergency nature of the military programme, resulting from the sudden decision to send a large army to France, the decentralization of army affairs, and the failure to prepare adequately in the years preceding entrance into the war — all these factors made a shortage of supplies in the training camps inevitable.

The first appropriation bill which was to provide the funds to purchase clothing, blankets, and other necessities was not passed until the 15th of June, leaving a pitifully brief space of time for the placing of contracts and the manufacture and transport of supplies. Many factories had to be built, and many delays resulted from the expansion of the Quartermaster Department, which had not been manned or equipped for such an emergency. The shortage of clothing was felt the more because of the extreme severity of the winter. After the initial difficulties had been passed supplies of this kind were furnished in profusion; but lack of preparation on the part of the War Department and the slowness of Congress to appropriate promptly produced a temporary situation of extreme discomfort and worse. The provision of food supplies was arranged more successfully. Soldiers would not be soldiers if they did not complain of their "chow." But the quality and variety of the food given to the new troops reached a higher degree than was reasonably to have been expected. The average soldier gained from ten to twelve pounds after entering the service. Provision was also made for his entertainment. Vaudeville, concerts, moving pictures formed an element of camp life, much to the surprise of the visiting French officers and Civil War veterans.

Americans naturally look back with pride to the making of their new army. The draft was accomplished smoothly and rapidly. Demonstrations against conscription, which in view of the Civil War draft riots had caused some apprehension, were almost unheard of and never serious. Of the three million called for service on the first draft, all but 150,000 were accounted for, and of those missing most were aliens who had left to enlist in their own armies. The problem of the slacker and of the conscientious objector, although vexatious, was never serious. The educative effect of the training upon the country was very considerable. All ranks and classes were gathered in, representing at least fifty-six different nationalities; artisans, millionaires, and hoboes bunked side by side; the youthful plutocrat saw life from a new angle, the wild mountaineer learned to read, the alien immigrant to speak English. Finally the purpose of the training was achieved, for America sent over a force that could fight successfully at the moment of crisis.

Amateur critics had assumed that the problem of raising an effective number of troops would prove far more difficult than that of producing the necessary equipment and munitions. It was generally believed that the industrial genius of America was such that American factories could provide all the artillery, small-arms, and aircraft that the armies could use. The most fantastic prophecies were indulged in. Experience showed, however, that it is easier to raise, train, and organize troops of superior sort in a brief period than it is to arm them. It stands as a matter of record that foreign artillery and machine guns alone made possible the attack on the St. Mihiel salient and the advance in the Argonne. As for military airplanes, had the Government relied upon those of American manufacture there would have been no American squadrons flying over the German lines previous to August, 1918, and not many between then and the signing of the armistice.

Such a statement should not imply blanket criticism of the Ordnance Department. The Government was perhaps slow, even after the United States entered the war, to realize the serious character of the military situation abroad and to appreciate the extent to which American aid would be necessary to allied victory. Hence the changes in the military programme which inevitably created confusion. But the decision to ensure against unforeseen disaster by preparing heavily for 1919 and 1920 and partially disregarding 1918 was based upon sound strategical reasoning. The war was brought to a close sooner than had been expected; hence the period of actual hostilities was devoted to laying down the foundations of a munitions industry, and the munitions actually produced, in the words of Assistant Secretary Crowell, "might almost be termed casual to the main enterprise, pilots of the quantities to come." Such a policy was possible because of the surplus production of the Allies. The latter stated that their production of artillery was such that they could equip all American divisions as they arrived in France during the year 1918.[1] This gave time "to build manufacturing capacity on a grand scale without the necessity of immediate production, time to secure the best in design, time to attain quality in the enormous outputs to come later as opposed to early quantities of indifferent class."

The lack of preparation in the matter of machine guns has received wide publicity. In this, as in artillery, the deficiency was made good by the Allies up to the final weeks of the war. In April, 1917, the army possessed only a small number of machine guns entirely inadequate even for the training of the new troops and half of which would not take American service cartridges. Less than seven hundred machine rifles were on hand. Manufacturing facilities for machine guns were limited; there were only two factories in the United States actually producing in quantity. Orders for four thousand

[1] As a result of the agreement thus made the United States shipped overseas between the time of the declaration of war and the signing of the armistice only 815 complete pieces of mobile artillery, including all produced for France and Great Britain as well as for American troops. Of the 75's only 181 complete units were shipped abroad, the American Expeditionary Force securing 1828 from the French. Of the 155 millimeter howitzers none of American manufacture reached the front. French deliveries amounted to 747.—*America's Munitions, 1917–1918* (Report of Benedict Crowell, Assistant Secretary of War), p. 90.

Vickers had been placed the preceding December, but deliveries had not been made by the beginning of April. Either because of jealousy in the department, or because of justifiable technical reasons, various experts demanded a better machine gun than any used by the Allies, and Secretary Baker took the responsibility of delaying matters so as to hold the competition recommended by a board of investigation. This competition was planned for May 1, 1917, with the result that we entered the war without having decided upon any type of machine gun, and it was not until some weeks later that the Browning was approved.

First deliveries of this gun could not be made until April, 1918, a year after the declaration of war. In the meantime, the War Department utilized existing facilities to the limit, and placed large orders for Colt, Lewis, and Vickers machine guns. But the heavy machine guns and automatic rifles used by our troops in the field were furnished by the French and the British until May, 1918. During that month and June the eleven American divisions that sailed were provided with American-made Vickers, although they still used the French-made Chauchat automatic rifles. After June, all American troops to sail received a full equipment of

Brownings, both heavy machine guns and automatic rifles. Altogether 27,000 heavy Brownings and 29,000 light Brownings were shipped to the American Expeditionary Force, sufficient by the time of the armistice to equip completely all the American troops in France. They were not used in combat until the Meuse-Argonne battle, where they amply justified the faith of General Pershing.

The policy of delaying production in order to obtain the best quality was not followed in the case of the rifle, and the results unquestionably justified the plan, ultimately adopted, of accepting a slightly inferior type which could be produced at once in quantity. The American army rifle, the Springfield, was generally regarded as the most accurate the world had seen. Unfortunately there was little hope of expanding the production of Springfields sufficiently to meet the necessities of the new National Army. For several years previous to 1917 the Government, with myopic vision, had cut down expenditures for the manufacture of small-arms and ammunition, with the result that artisans skilled in making Springfields had been scattered. Even if the two factories that had been turning out Springfields could be restaffed, their combined production would be insufficient. Private plants could not be utilized for early quantity production, because of the time that would be taken in building up an adequate manufacturing equipment and training the artisans. Fortune intervened. It happened that three large American firms were about to complete important contracts for supplying Enfield rifles to the British Government. Their plants and skilled labor might be turned to account, but the Enfield was not regarded as satisfactory, principally because its ammunition was inferior to that taken by the Springfield. The War Department decided to attempt a change in the bore of the Enfield so that it would use Springfield cartridges, and to make other minor simplifications and improvements. The experiment proved successful to the highest degree. The modified Enfields were reported to be only slightly inferior to the Springfields and by the end of December, 1917, five thousand a day were being turned out. Altogether American manufactories produced during the war about two and a half million rifles, of which all but three hundred thousand were modified Enfields.

In the matter of airplane production the record is far less satisfactory. It is, perhaps, too early to distribute with justice the blame for the delays in production, and full cognizance should be taken of the difficulties which had to be overcome. But whatever explanations are to be found, it is an undeniable fact that not until August, 1918, three months before the armistice, was an American squadron equipped with American planes. The Allies had looked to America for the production of combat planes in quantity and Congress, responding to popular enthusiasm, had in the first days of the war appropriated more than half a billion dollars for their manufacture. An Aircraft Production Board was organized, with Howard E. Coffin as chairman, although the actual manufacture of the machines was under the supervision of the Signal Corps. Promises were made that by the spring of 1918 the Germans would be completely at the mercy of American airmen.

But difficulties developed. A new type of motor had to be produced, capable of serving in any kind of airplane; this was rapidly and successfully accomplished, and in July, 1917, the Liberty Motor was approved. But just as manufacturing was about to begin changes in the design were demanded, with ensuing delays. There was confusion between the jurisdiction of the Aircraft Board and that of the Signal Corps. The organization of the latter was less efficient than had been expected, and men who knew little or nothing of the technique of aircraft were placed in charge of production. When orders were given for planes to be constructed in France, seven thousand American machinists had to be sent over to release the French machinists who were to work on these contracts, with consequent delays to American production. Repeated alterations in the designs of airplanes must be made to meet changing requirements sent from the front, and large numbers of planes almost ready for delivery had to be scrapped. Two of the types manufactured proved to be unsatisfactory and were condemned, with an estimated loss of twenty-six million dollars. Finally the bitter cold of the winter made it difficult to secure the indispensable spruce from the northwestern forests, and lumbering operations were hampered by extensive strikes, which were said to have resulted from German intrigues.

General disappointment at the failure to produce airplanes in quantity by the spring of 1918 was the more bitter because of the high hopes that had been aroused by those in authority. Instead of confessing the serious nature of the delays, the War Department attempted to conceal not merely the mistakes made but the fact that airplanes could not possibly reach France in any numbers before the autumn of 1918. Thus when at last, in February, a single combat plane was completed and shipped, the War Department issued the statement: "The first American-built battle planes are to-day *en route* to France. This first shipment, although not in itself large, marks the final overcoming of many difficulties met in building up a new and intricate industry." When General Wood returned from France in March and reported that not one American-built plane was in action there, and when the Senate investigation committee unearthed the existence of all the delays, the disillusioned public gave vent to fierce criticism. It was to some extent calmed by the appointment, in April, of John D. Ryan, of the Anaconda Copper Company, as director of aircraft production for the army. By this time many of the most serious difficulties had been passed. When the armistice was signed about twelve thousand airplanes had been produced by American plants, of which a third were service-planes.[1]

It is impossible here to trace the activities of the various departments in the herculean task of arming the nation. But one should not forget that

[1] Ayres, *The War with Germany*, 87-90.

there was much which never received wide publicity. The development of ordnance carried with it the manufacture of quantities of ammunition hitherto undreamt of, the building of railway and motorized artillery, the improvement of sight and fire-control apparatus, the making of all sorts of trench-warfare *matériel*. The Air Service had to concern itself with the manufacture of radio telephones, armament for airplanes, the synchronizing of machine guns to fire through propeller blades, airplane bombs, air photography, and pyrotechnics. The Chemical Warfare Service was busy with the making of toxic gases and gas defense equipment, using the peach stones and cocoanut shells which every one was asked to save. The enormous quantities of medical and dental supplies must be gathered by the Quartermaster Department, which also had charge of the salvage service and the thousand gargantuan household occupations, such as laundering and incineration of garbage, that went with the maintenance of the army in camp. The Signal Corps must produce wire, telegraphs, telephones, switchboards, radio equipment, batteries, field glasses, photographic outfits, and carrier pigeons.

Upon its navy the United States has always relied chiefly for defense and in this branch of the service the country was better prepared for war in 1917 than in the army. Indeed when the nation entered the struggle many persons believed that the sole practical fighting assistance the United States should give the Allies would be upon the sea. Josephus Daniels, the Secretary of the Navy, was a Southern politician, of limited administrative experience and capacity. During the first years of his appointment he had alienated navy officers through the introduction of pet reforms and his frank advocacy of a little navy. Resiliency, however, was one of his characteristics and he followed President Wilson in 1916, when the latter demanded from Congress authority for an expansion in the navy which seemed only prudent in view of international conditions. Largely owing to the efforts of the Assistant Secretary, Franklin D. Roosevelt, the months immediately preceding the declaration of war witnessed strenuous preparations to render aid to the Allies in case the United States should participate. Thereafter Secretary Daniels tended to sink his personality and judgment in the conduct of the naval war and to defer to the opinion of various officers, of whom Admiral William S. Benson, Chief of Naval Operations, was the most influential. When war was declared two flotillas of destroyers were at once sent to Queenstown to assist in chasing and sinking submarines, and were placed under the command of Admiral William S. Sims. Battleships and cruisers followed, though by no means with the expedition nor in the numbers desired by Sims, who believed that by using practically the entire naval force at once the submarine could be exterminated and the war ended.

At home, the Navy Department entered upon a process of expansion which increased its personnel from 65,000 to 497,000 when the armistice was signed. A rapid development in naval construction was planned, with emphasis upon destroyers. The effects of this programme became visible within a year; during the first nine months of 1918 no less than eighty-three destroyers were launched, as against sixty-two for the preceding nine years. Submarine chasers of a special design were built and many private yachts taken over and adapted to the war against the submarine. During the course of the war two battleships and twenty-eight submarines were completed. Expansion in naval shipbuilding plans was paralleled by the construction of giant docks; by camps sufficient for the training of two hundred thousand men; and by a naval aircraft factory from which a seaplane was turned out seven months after work on the factory was begun. Naval aviators returning from the Channel coasts superintended flying schools and undertook the patrol of our Atlantic seaboard.

If much of these military preparations was not translated into accomplishment before the war ended, it was because the United States was preparing wisely for a long struggle and it seemed necessary that the foundations should be broad and deep. "America was straining her energies towards a goal," said the Director of Munitions, "toward the realization of an ambition which, in the production of munitions, dropped the year 1918 almost out of consideration altogether, which indeed did not bring the full weight of American men and *matériel* into the struggle even in 1919, but which left it for 1920, if the enemy had not yet succumbed to the growing American power, to witness the maximum strength of the United States in the field." It was the knowledge of this preparation which, to some extent, helped to convince the German General Staff of the futility of further resistance and thus to bring the war to an early end.

The dependence of the United States upon the

Allies for equipment and munitions does not deserve the vitriolic anathemas of certain critics. The country did not enter the struggle as if it expected to fight the war single-handed. Distribution of labor and supplies between the United States and the Allies was merely a wise and economic measure. At their own request, the Allies were furnished with that which they most needed — money, food, and man-power. In return they provided the United States with the artillery and machine guns which they could spare and which they could manufacture more cheaply and rapidly. Finally there is the outstanding fact, of which America may always be proud, that this heterogeneous democracy, organized, so far as organization existed, for the pursuits of peace, was able in the space of sixteen months, to provide an army capable of fighting successfully one of the most difficult campaigns of the war, and that which led directly to the military defeat of Germany.

The ultimate success of President Wilson's war policies could hardly have been achieved except by the process of centralization which he never lost from view. His insistence upon centralized responsibility and control in political matters was paralleled in the military field. Nothing illustrates this principle better than the centralization of the American Expeditionary Force under the absolute and unquestioned command of General Pershing. The latter was given free rein. The jealousies which so weakened the Union armies during the first years of the Civil War were ruthlessly repressed. No generals were sent to France of whom he did not approve. When the Allies threatened to appeal to Washington over Pershing's head, President Wilson turned a deaf ear.

In the United States, the President sought similar centralization through the General Staff. It was this body which prepared the different plans for the Draft Act, the Pershing expedition, and finally for the gigantic task of putting a million men in France by the summer of 1918. To the staff was given the formulation of the training programme along the lines recommended by Pershing. Always, however, it was hampered by the multiple responsibility that characterized the old-style army machine with its bureau chiefs competing with each other, with the navy, and with the Allies. Quartermaster Department, Ordnance Department, Signal Corps, and the other bureaus were uncoördinated, and inevitable waste and inefficiency followed all their operations. It was the crisis that arose from the problem of supplies, in the winter of 1917, that furnished the President with the opportunity to cut red-tape and secure the centralization he desired. That opportunity came with the blanket powers bestowed upon him by the Overman Act, the full significance of which can only be appreciated after a consideration of the measures taken to centralize the industrial resources of the nation.

CHAPTER VII

THE HOME FRONT

On May 18, 1917, President Wilson issued a proclamation in which are to be found the following significant sentences:

In the sense in which we have been wont to think of armies there are no armies in this struggle, there are entire nations armed. Thus, the men who remain to till the soil and man the factories are no less a part of the army that is in France than the men beneath the battle flags. It must be so with us. It is not an army that we must shape and train for war — it is a Nation. To this end our people must draw close in one compact front against a common foe. But this cannot be if each man pursues a private purpose. All must pursue one purpose. The Nation needs all men, but it needs each man, not in the field that will most pleasure him, but in the endeavor that will best serve the common good. Thus, though a sharpshooter pleases to operate a trip-hammer for the forging of great guns, and an expert machinist desires to march with the flag, the Nation is being served only when the sharpshooter marches and the machinist remains at his levers. The whole

Nation must be a team, in which each man shall play the part for which he is best fitted.

If President Wilson deserves severe criticism for his failure to endorse adequate plans of preparation for war while his country was at peace, he should be given due credit for his appreciation that the home front must be organized if the fighting front was to be victorious. He perceived clearly that it was necessary to carry into the industrial life of the nation that centralizing process which characterized his military policy. That the nation at home was made to feel itself part of the fighting forces and coöperated enthusiastically and effectively in the organization of the national resources was not the least of the triumphs of the United States. Such organization demanded great sacrifice, not merely of luxuries or comforts, but of settled habits, which are difficult to break. It must necessarily be of an emergency character, for the United States possessed no bureaucratic system like that which obtains on the continent of Europe for the centralization of trade, manufactures, food production, and the thousand activities that form part of economic life. But the event proved that both the spirit and the brains of the American people were equal to the crisis.

The problem of coördinating the national industries for the supply of the army was complicated by the military decentralization described in the preceding chapter, which President Wilson was not able to remedy before the final months of the war. The army did not form or state its requirements as one body but through five supply bureaus, which acted independently and in competition with each other. Bids for materials from the different bureaus conflicted with each other, with those of the navy, and of the Allies. Not merely was it essential that such demands should be coördinated, but that some central committee should be able to say how large was the total supply of any sort of materials, how soon they could be produced, and to prevent the waste of such materials in unessential production. If the army was decentralized, American industry as a whole was in a state of complete chaos, so far as any central organization was concerned. On the side of business every firm in every line of production was competing in the manufacture of essential and unessential articles, in transportation, and in bidding for and holding the necessary labor. Mr. Wilson set himself the task of evolving order out of this chaos.

The President, as in the purely military problem

where he utilized the General Staff as his instrument, prepared to adapt existing machinery, rather than to create a completely new organization. For a time he seems to have believed that his Cabinet might serve the function. But it was ill-adapted to handle the sort of problems that must be solved. It was composed of men chosen largely for political reasons, and despite much public complaint it had not been strengthened after Wilson's reëlection. Franklin K. Lane, the Secretary of the Interior, was generally recognized as a man of excellent business judgment, willing to listen to experts, and capable of coöperating effectively with the economic leaders of the country. His influence with the President, however, seemed to be overshadowed by that of Newton D. Baker and William G. McAdoo, Secretaries of War and of the Treasury, who had inspired the distrust of most business men. McAdoo in particular alienated financial circles because of his apparent suspicion of banking interest, and both, by their appeals to laboring men, laid themselves open to the charge of demagogic tactics. Robert Lansing, the Secretary of State, had won recognition as an expert international lawyer of long experience, but he could not be expected to exercise great influence, inasmuch as the

President obviously intended to remain his own foreign secretary. Albert S. Burleson, Postmaster-General, was a politician, expert in the minor tactics of party, whose conduct of the postal and telegraphic systems was destined to bring a storm of protest upon the entire Administration. Thomas W. Gregory, the Attorney-General, had gained entrance into the Cabinet by means of a railroad suit which had roused the ire of the transportation interests. The other members were, at that time, little known or spoken of. Wilson spent much time and effort in defending his Cabinet members from attacks, and yet it was believed that he rarely appealed to them for advice in the formulation of policies. Thus the Cabinet as a whole lacked the very qualities essential to a successful organizing committee: ability to secure the coöperation and respect of the industrial leaders of the country.

Titular functions of an organizing character, nevertheless, had been conferred upon six members of the Cabinet in August, 1916, through the creation of a "Council of National Defense"; they were charged with the "coördination of industries and resources for the national security and welfare." The actual labor of coördination, however, was to be exercised by an advisory commission of seven, which included Howard E. Coffin, in charge of munitions, Daniel Willard, president of the Baltimore and Ohio Railroad, in charge of transportation, Julius Rosenwald, president of the Sears-Roebuck Company, in charge of supplies including clothing, Bernard M. Baruch, a versatile financial trader, in charge of metals, minerals, and raw materials, Samuel Gompers, president of the American Federation of Labor, in charge of labor and the welfare of workers, Hollis Godfrey in charge of engineering and education, and Franklin H. Martin in charge of medicine. The commission at once prepared to lay down its programme, to create sub-committees and technical boards, and to secure the assistance of business leaders, without whose coöperation their task could not be fulfilled.

Following plans developed by the Council of National Defense, experts in every business likely to prove of importance were called upon to coördinate and stimulate war necessities, to control their distribution, to provide for the settlement of disputes between employers and wage-earners, to fix prices, to conserve resources. Scientific and technical experts were directed in their researches. The General Medical Board and the Committee on Engineering and Education were supervised in their mobilization of doctors and surgeons, engineers, physicists and chemists, professors and graduate students in the university laboratories. Everywhere and in all lines experience and brains were sought and utilized. State Councils of Defense were created to oversee the work of smaller units and to establish an effective means of communication between the individual and the national Government. Naturally much over-organization resulted and some waste of time and energy; but the universal spirit of voluntary coöperation evoked by the Councils overbalanced this loss and aided greatly in putting the country on an effective war basis. As Wilson said, "beyond all question the highest and best form of efficiency is the spontaneous coöperation of a free people." In return for their efforts the people received an education in public spirit and civic consciousness such as could have come in no other way.

Of the committees of the Council, that on munitions developed along the most elaborate lines, becoming of such importance that on July 28, 1917, it was reorganized as the War Industries Board. As such it gradually absorbed most of the functions of the Council which were not transferred to other agencies of the Government. During the autumn of 1917 the activities of the Board underwent rapid extension, but it lacked the power to enforce its decisions. As in the case of the General Staff, it was important that it should have authority not merely to plan but also to supervise and execute. Such a development was foreshadowed in the reorganization of the Board in March, 1918, under the chairmanship of Bernard M. Baruch, and when the President received the blanket authority conferred by the Overman Act, he immediately invested the War Industries Board with the centralizing power which seemed so necessary. Henceforth it exercised an increasingly strict control over all the industries of the country.

The purpose of the Board was, generally speaking, to secure for the Government and the Allies the goods essential for making war successfully, and to protect the civil needs of the country. The supply of raw materials to the manufacturer as well as the delivery of finished products was closely regulated by a system of priorities. The power of the Board in its later development was dictatorial, inasmuch as it might discipline any refractory producer or manufacturer by the withdrawal of the assignments he expected. The leaders of each of the more important industries were called into council, in order to determine resources and needs, and the degree of preference to which each industry was entitled. Some were especially favored, in order to stimulate production in a line that was of particular importance or was failing to meet the exigencies of the military situation; shipments to others of a less essential character were deferred. Committees of the Board studied industrial conditions and recommended the price that should be fixed for various commodities; stability was thus artificially secured and profiteering lessened. The Conservation Division worked out and enforced methods of standardizing patterns in order to economize materials and labor. The Steel Division coöperated with the manufacturers for the speeding-up of production; and the Chemical Division, among other duties, stimulated the vitally important supply of potash, dyes, and nitrates. Altogether it has been roughly estimated that the industrial capacity of the country was increased by twenty per cent through the organizing labors and authority of the War Industries Board.

The success of this Board would have been impossible without the building up of an extraordinary *esprit de corps* among the men who were brought face to face with these difficult problems of industry and commerce. Their chairman relied, of course, upon the coöperation of the leaders of "big business," who now, in the hour of the country's need, sank their prejudice against governmental interference and gave freely of their experience, brains, and administrative power. Men whose incomes were measured in the hundreds of thousands forgot their own business and worked at Washington on a salary of a dollar a year.

The same spirit of coöperation was evoked when it came to the conservation and the production of food. If steel was to win the war, its burden could not be supported without wheat, and for some months in 1917 and 1918 victory seemed to depend largely upon whether the Allies could find enough to eat. Even in normal times Great Britain and France import large quantities of foodstuffs; under war conditions they were necessarily dependent upon foreign grain-producing countries. The surplus grain of the Argentine and Australia was not available because of the length of the voyage and the scarcity of shipping; the Russian wheat supply was cut off by enemy control of the Dardanelles even before it was dissipated by corrupt officials or reckless revolutionaries. The Allies, on the verge of starvation, therefore looked to North America.

Yet the stock of cereals when the United States entered the war was at a lower level than it had been
for years and the number of food animals had also
been reduced.

To meet the crisis President Wilson called upon
one of the most interesting and commanding personalities of modern times. Herbert Clark Hoover was
a Californian mining engineer, of broad experience
in Australia, China, and England, who in 1914 had
been given control of Allied Relief abroad. The following year he undertook the difficult and delicate
task of organizing food relief for Belgium. He was
able to arouse the enthusiastic sympathy of Americans, win financial support on a large scale, procure
the much-needed food, and provide for its effective
distribution among the suffering Belgians, in spite
of the suspicions of the Germans and the hindrances
thrown in his path. A master organizer, with keen
flair for efficient subordinates, of broad vision never
muddied by details, with sound knowledge of business economics, and a gift for dramatic appeal,
Hoover was ideally fitted to conduct the greatest
experiment in economic organization the world had
seen. Unsentimental himself, he knew how to
arouse emotion — a necessary quality, since the
food problem demanded heavy personal sacrifices

which would touch every individual; brusque in manner, he avoided giving the offense which naturally follows any interference with the people's dinner and which would destroy the essential spirit of voluntary coöperation.

Five days after the declaration of war, President Wilson, through the Council of National Defense, named a committee on food supply, with Hoover at its head, and shortly thereafter named him food commissioner. Hoover began his work of educating the people to realize the necessity of economy and extra-production; but he lacked the administrative powers which were essential if his work was to prove effective, and it was not until August that Congress passed the Lever Act which provided for strict control of food under an administrator. This measure encountered strong opposition in the Senate and from the farmers, who feared lest the provisions against hoarding of food would prevent them from holding their products for high prices. Wilson exerted his personal influence vigorously for the bill in the face of congressional opposition, which demanded that large powers of control should be given to a Senate committee of ten, and he was finally successful in his appeal. He thereupon appointed Hoover Food Administrator with practically unlimited powers, legalizing the work already begun on his own initiative.

Hoover at once made arrangements to prevent the storage of wheat in large quantities and to eliminate speculative dealings in wheat on the grain exchanges. He then offered to buy the entire wheat crop at a fair price and agreed with the millers to take flour at a fair advance on the price of wheat. Fearful lest the farmers should be discouraged from planting the following year, 1918, he offered to buy all the wheat that could be raised at two dollars a bushel. If peace came before the crop was disposed of, the Government might be compelled to take over the wheat at a higher price than the market, but the offer was a necessary inducement to extensive planting. In the meantime Hoover appealed to the country to utilize every scrap of ground for the growing of food products. Every one of whatever age and class turned gardener. The spacious and perfectly trimmed lawns of the wealthy, as well as the weed-infested back yards of the poor, were dug up and planted with potatoes or corn. Community gardens flourished in the villages and outside of the larger towns, where men, women, and children came out in the evening, after their regular work, to labor with rake and hoe. There were perhaps two million "war gardens" over and beyond the already established gardens, which unquestionably enabled many a citizen to reduce his daily demands on the grocer, and stimulated his interest in the problem of food conservation. As a result of Hoover's dealing with the farmers, during the year 1917 the planted wheat acreage exceeded the average of the preceding five years by thirty-five million acres, or by about twelve per cent, and another additional five million acres were planted in 1918. The result was the largest wheat crop in American history except that of 1915, despite the killing cold of the winter of 1917 and the withering drought of the summer of 1918. An increase in the number of live stock was also secured and the production of milk, meat, and wool showed a notable development.

Hoover achieved equal success in the problem of conserving food. He realized that he must bring home to the individual housewife the need of the closest economy, and he organized a nation-wide movement to secure voluntary pledges that the rules and requests of the Food Administration would be observed. People were asked to use other flours than wheat whenever possible, to be sparing of sugar and meat, to utilize substitutes, and rigidly to avoid waste. On every billboard and in all the newspapers were to be seen appeals to save food. Housewives were enrolled as "members of the Food Administration" and were given placards to post in their windows announcing their membership and the willingness of the family to abide by its requests. Certain days of the week were designated as "wheatless" or "meatless" when voluntary demi-fasts were to be observed, the nonobservance of which spelled social ostracism. To "Hooverize" became a national habit, and children were denied a spoonful of sugar on their cereal, "because Mr. Hoover would not like it." Hoover, with his broad forehead, round face, compelling eyes, and underhung jaw, became the benevolent bogey of the nation. It was a movement of general renunciation such as no country had undergone except at the pinch of biting necessity.[1] In the meantime prices were prevented from rapid increase by a system of licenses, which tended to prevent hoarding or speculation. Attempts to capitalize the need of the world for private gain, or in common parlance, to

[1] Restaurants and hotels coöperated; during a period of only two months they were reported as having saved nine thousand tons of meat, four thousand tons of flour, and a thousand tons of sugar. City garbage plants announced a decrease in the amount of garbage collected ranging from ten to thirteen per cent.

"profiteer," were comparatively rare and were adequately punished by revocation of license or by forced sale of hoardings.

As a result of the organization of food supply, the stimulation of production, and the prevention of waste, America was able to save the Entente nations, and, later, much of central and southeastern Europe from starvation, without herself enduring anything worse than discomfort. The Government was able at the same time to provide the troops in France with food which, to the *poilus* at least, seemed luxurious. When the United States entered the war the country was prepared to export 20,000,000 bushels of wheat; instead it sent over 141,000,000. In four months, in the summer of 1918, the American people saved out of their regular consumption and sent abroad half a million tons of sugar. The autumn of 1918 saw an increase of nearly a million tons of pork products over what was available the previous year. Altogether, during the crop year of 1918, America doubled the average amount of food sent to Europe immediately before the war, notwithstanding unfavorable weather conditions and the congestion of freight that resulted from other war necessities. The total contribution in foodstuffs exported to

Europe that year amounted to a value of about two billion dollars. This was done without food cards and with a minimum of edicts. It was the work of education and conscience.

Fuel like food was a war necessity and there was equal need of stimulating production by assuring a fair profit and of eliminating all possible waste. Without the steam power provided by coal, raw materials could not be transformed into the manufactured articles demanded by military necessity, nor distributed by the railroads and steamships. Soon after the declaration of war, a committee of coal operators, meeting under the authorization of the Council of National Defense, drew up a plan for the stimulation of coal production and its more economical distribution. This committee voluntarily set a price for coal lower than the current market price, in order to prevent a rise in manufacturing costs; it was approved by the Secretary of the Interior, who warmly praised the spirit of sacrifice displayed by the operators. Unfortunately the Secretary of War, as chairman of the Council of National Defense, repudiated the arrangement, on the ground that the price agreed upon was too high. The operators were discouraged, because of the difficulty of stimulating

production under the lower price which Secretary
Baker insisted upon; they were further disappointed at the postponement of plans for a zone system
and an elimination of long cross hauls, designed to
relieve the load that would be thrown upon railroad
transportation in the coming winter.

In August, Wilson was empowered by the Lever
Act to appoint a Fuel Administrator and chose
Harry A. Garfield, President of Williams College.
Conditions, however, became more confused. The
fuel problem was one of transportation quite as
much as of production; the railroads were unable
to furnish the needed coal-cars, and because of an
expensive and possibly unfair system of car allot-
ment, coal distribution was hampered. Add to
this the fact that numerous orders for coal shipments had been deferred until autumn, in the belief
that the Administration, which in the person of
Baker was not believed to look on the coal operators with favor, would enforce low prices. Hence
during the last three months of the year an un-
precedented amount of coal had to be shipped, and
the congestion on the competing railroads was such
that the country faced a real coal famine. In
December, the Government recognized the obvious
fact that the railroad must be placed under one

management, if the confusion in the whole industrial situation were to be eliminated. President Wilson accordingly announced that the Federal Government would take over the railroads for the period of the war.

This measure came too late to save the country from the evil effects of the fuel shortage. The penalty for the delays of the preceding summer had to be paid, and it was the heavier because of the severity of the winter. Overloaded trains were stalled and harbors froze over, imprisoning the coal barges. Thirty-seven ships laden with essential military supplies were held up in New York harbor for lack of fuel, and long strings of empties blocked the sidings, while the shippers all over the country cried for cars. To meet the crisis Garfield decreed that all manufacturing plants east of the Mississippi should be shut down for five days and for a series of Mondays, until the 25th of March. The order applied also to places of amusement, private offices, and most stores, which were not allowed to furnish heat. Munitions plants and essential industries, as well as Government offices were naturally excepted. "Heatless Mondays" caused great inconvenience and bitter criticism, for they came at the moment when it was most important that the economic life of the nation should be functioning at its greatest efficiency. But the embargo helped to tide over the crisis. As in the case of food, the public, once it appreciated the necessity of the situation, accepted it cheerfully. Domestic economy was also widely preached and applied, to the slogan, "Save a shovelful of coal a day." The elimination of electric advertisements and the diminution of street lighting, served to lessen the non-essential demand for coal; and the crisis also forced the introduction of "daylight saving," the advancement of the clock by an hour, during the months extending from March to October, thus saving artificial light.

In the meantime the Fuel Administration, the operators, and the miners were coöperating to increase coal production. The enthusiasm of the mine workers was stimulated by making them realize that they were indeed part of the fighting forces. A competitive spirit was aroused and mining conditions were bettered to keep them satisfied. Labor responded to the call. Holidays were omitted and emulation between different shifts became keen.[1] Increased production was

[1] In 1918 the average number of days worked by each miner in the bituminous fields was greater by twelve than that of 1917,

paralleled by more efficient distribution. A zone system, finally put into operation, eliminated approximately 160,000,000 car miles. Local fuel administrators kept in constant touch with the need of the localities under their jurisdiction, studied methods of abolishing unnecessary manufacturing use of coal and refused coal to non-essential industries.

Similar increase in the production and saving of oil was accomplished. The oil-burning vessels of the allied navies and merchant marines, the motor transport service of the armies, all made this necessary. In 1918 the production of oil in the United States was fourteen per cent greater than in 1914. In response to an urgent cable from Marshal Foch, which ran: "If you don't keep up your petrol supply we shall lose the war," a series of "gasless Sundays" was suggested. For nearly two months, merely at the request of the Fuel Administration and without any compulsion except that arising from public opinion, Sunday motoring was practically abandoned. That most crowded of motor

---

and by twenty-five than that of 1916. During the half-year period from April to September, 1918, bituminous production was twelve per cent greater than in the corresponding period of the previous year, which had itself established a record, despite the decrease in the number of mine workers.

thoroughfares, the Boston Post Road from New York to Stamford, might have served as playground for a kindergarten. The estimated saving of gasoline amounted to a million barrels: about four per cent of the gasoline sent abroad in 1918 was provided by the gasless Sundays.

Credit must be given the Fuel Administration for the large measure of success which it finally secured. It was slow in its early organization and at first failed to make full use of the volunteer committees of coal operators and labor representatives who offered their assistance and whose experience qualified them to give invaluable advice. But Garfield showed his capacity for learning the basic facts of the situation, and ultimately chose strong advisers. When he entered upon his duties he found the crisis so far advanced that it could not be immediately solved. Furthermore, in a situation which demanded the closest coöperation between the Fuel and the Railroad Administration, he did not always receive the assistance from the latter which he had a right to expect.

As a war measure, the temporary nationalization of the railroads was probably necessary. Whatever the ultimate advantages of private ownership and the system of competition, during the period of military necessity perfect coördination was essential. Railroad facilities could not be improved because new equipment, so far as it could be manufactured, had to be sent abroad; the only solution of the problem of congestion seemed to be an improvement of service. During the first nine months after the declaration of war a notable increase in the amount of freight carried was effected; nevertheless, as winter approached, it became obvious that the roads were not operating as a unit and could not carry the load demanded of them. Hence resulted the appointment of McAdoo in December, 1917, as Director-General, with power to operate all the railroads as a single line.

During the spring of 1918 the Administration gradually overcame the worst of the transportation problems. To the presidents and management of the various railroads must go the chief share of credit for the successful accomplishment of this titanic task. Despite their distrust of McAdoo and their objections to his methods, they coöperated loyally with the Railroad Administration in putting through the necessary measures of coördination and in the elimination of the worst features of the former competitive system. They adopted a permit system which prevented the loading of freight unless it could be unloaded at its destination; they insisted upon more rapid unloading of cars; they consolidated terminals to facilitate the handling of cars; they curtailed circuitous routing of freight; they reduced the use of Pullman cars for passenger service. As a result, after May, 1918, congestion was diminished and during the summer was no longer acute. This was accomplished despite the number of troops moved, amounting during the first ten months of 1918 to six and a half millions. In addition the railroads carried large quantities of food, munitions, building materials for cantonments, and other supplies, most of which converged upon eastern cities and ports. The increase in the number of grain-carrying cars alone, from July to November, was 135,000 over the same period of the previous year.

Unquestionably the Government's administration of the railroads has a darker side. Complaints were frequent that the Railroad Administration sacrificed other interests for its own advantage. The future of the roads was said not to be carefully safeguarded, and equipment and rolling stock mishandled and allowed to deteriorate. Above all, at the moment when it was quite as essential to preserve the morale of labor on the home front as that of the troops in France, McAdoo made concessions to labor that were more apt to destroy discipline and *esprit de corps* than to maintain them. The authority given for the unionization of railroad employees, the stopping of piecework, the creation of shop committees, weakened the control of the foremen and led to a loss of shop efficiency which has been estimated at thirty per cent. Government control was necessary, but in the form in which it came it proved costly.

During the months when manufacturing plants were built and their output speeded up, when fuel and food were being produced in growing amounts, when the stalled freight trains were being disentangled, there was unceasing call for ocean-going tonnage. Food and war materials would be of little use unless the United States had the ships in which to transport them across the Atlantic. The Allies sorely needed American help to replace the tonnage sunk by German submarines; during some months, Allied shipping was being destroyed at the rate of six million tons a year. Furthermore if an effective military force were to be transported to France, according to the plans that germinated in the summer of 1917, there would be need of every possible cubic inch of tonnage. The entire military situation hinged upon the shipping problem. Yet when the United States joined in war on Germany there was not a shipyard in the country which would accept a new order; every inch of available space was taken by the navy or private business.

In September, 1916, the United States Shipping Board had been organized to operate the Emergency Fleet Corporation, which had been set up primarily to develop trade with South America. This body now prepared a gigantic programme of shipbuilding, which expanded as the need for tonnage became more evident. By November 15, 1917, the Board planned for 1200 ships with dead weight tonnage of seven and a half millions. The difficulties of building new yards, of collecting trained workmen and technicians were undoubtedly great, but they might have been overcome more easily had not unfortunate differences developed between William Denman, the chairman of the Board, who advocated wooden ships, and General George W. Goethals, the head of the Emergency Fleet Corporation, who depended upon steel construction. The differences led to the resignation of both and continued disorganization hampered the rapid fulfillment of the programme.

Edward N. Hurley became chairman of the Shipping Board, but it was not until the spring of 1918, when Charles M. Schwab of the Bethlehem Steel Company was put in charge of the Emergency Fleet Corporation as Director General of shipbuilding, that public confidence in ultimate success seemed justified.

Much of the work accomplished during the latter days of the war was spectacular. Waste lands along the Delaware overgrown with weeds were transformed within a year into a shipyard with twenty-eight ways, a ship under construction on each one, with a record of fourteen ships already launched. The spirit of the workmen was voiced by the placard that hung above the bulletin board announcing daily progress, which proclaimed, "Three ships a week or bust." The Hog Island yards near Philadelphia and the Fore River yards in Massachusetts became great cities with docks, sidings, shops, offices, and huge stacks of building materials. Existing yards, such as those on the Great Lakes, were enlarged so that in fourteen months they sent to the ocean a fleet of 181 steel vessels. The new ships were standardized and built on the "fabricated" system, which provided for the manufacture of the various parts in different factories and their assembling at the shipyards. In a single day, July 4, 1918, there were launched in American shipyards ninety-five vessels, with a dead weight tonnage of 474,464. In one of the Great Lakes yards a 5500 ton steel freighter was launched seventeen days after the keel was laid, and seventeen days later was delivered to the Shipping Board, complete and ready for service.

This work was not accomplished without tremendous expenditure and much waste. The Shipping Board was careless in its financial management and unwise in many of its methods. By introducing the cost plus system in the letting of contracts it fostered extravagance and waste and increased and intensified the industrial evils that had resulted from its operation in the building of army cantonments. The contractors received the cost of construction plus a percentage commission; obviously they had no incentive to economize; the greater the expense the larger their commission. Hence they willingly paid exorbitant prices for materials and agreed to "fancy" wages. Not merely was the expense of securing the necessary tonnage multiplied, but the cost of materials and labor in all other industries was seriously enhanced. The high wages paid tended to destroy the patriotic spirit of the shipworkers, who were enticed by greed rather than by the glory of service. The effect on drafted soldiers was bound to be unfortunate, for they could not but realize the injustice of a system which gave them low pay for risking their lives, while their friends in the shipyards received fabulous wages. Such aspects of the early days of the Shipping Board were ruthlessly reformed by Schwab when he took control of the Emergency Fleet Corporation. Appealing to the patriotism of the workers he reduced costs and increased efficiency, according to some critics, by thirty per cent, according to others, by no less than one hundred and ten per cent.

By September, 1918, the Shipping Board had brought under its jurisdiction 2600 vessels with a total dead weight tonnage of more than ten millions. Of this fleet, sixteen per cent had been built by the Emergency Fleet Corporation. The remainder was represented by ships which the Board had requisitioned when America entered the war, by the ships of Allied and neutral countries which had been purchased and chartered, and by interned enemy ships which had been seized. The last-named were damaged by their crews at the time of the declaration of war, but were fitted for service with little delay by a new process of electric welding. Such German boats as the *Vaterland*, rechristened the *Leviathan*, and the *George Washington*, together with smaller ships, furnished half a million tons of German cargo-space. The ships which transported American soldiers were not chiefly provided by the Shipping Board, more than fifty per cent being represented by boats borrowed from Great Britain.[1]

More effective use of shipping was fostered by the War Trade Board, which had been created six months after the declaration of war by the Trading with the Enemy Act (October 6, 1917), and which, in conjunction with the activities of the Alien Property Custodian, possessed full powers to curtail enemy trade. It thereby obtained practical control of the foreign commerce of this country, and was able both to conserve essential products for American use and to secure and economize tonnage.

Such control was assured through a system of

[1] In the last six months of the war over 1,500,000 men were carried abroad as follows:

        44 per cent in United States ships
        51 per cent in British ships
        3 per cent in Italian ships
        2 per cent in French ships

The United States transports included 450,000 tons of German origin; 300,000 tons supplied by commandeered Dutch boats; and 718,000 tons provided by the Emergency Fleet Corporation.

licenses for exports and imports. No goods could be shipped into or out of the country without a license, which was granted by the War Trade Board only after investigation of the character of the shipment and its destination or source. The earlier export of goods which had found their way to Germany through neutral countries was thus curtailed and the blockade on Germany became strangling. Products necessary to military effectiveness were secured from neutral states in return for permission to buy essentials here. Two millions of tonnage were obtained from neutral states for the use of the United States and Great Britain. Trade in non-essentials with the Orient and South America was limited, extra bottoms were thus acquired, and the production of non-essentials at home discouraged. Altogether, the War Trade Board exercised tremendous powers which, however necessary, might have provoked intense resentment in business circles; but these powers were enforced with a tact and discretion characteristic of the head of the Board, Vance McCormick, who was able successfully to avoid the irritation that might have been expected from such governmental interference with freedom of commerce.

The problem of labor was obviously one that must be faced by each of the war boards or administrations, and nearly all of them were compelled to establish some sort of labor division or tribunal within each separate field. The demands made upon the labor market by war industry were heavy, for the withdrawal of labor into the army created an inevitable scarcity at the moment when production must be increased, and the different industries naturally were brought to bid against each other; the value of any wage scale was constantly affected by the rising prices, while the introduction of inexperienced workmen and women affected the conditions of piecework, so that the question of wages and conditions of labor gave rise to numerous discussions. The Labor Committee of the Council of National Defense had undertaken to meet such problems as early as February, 1917, but it was not until the beginning of the next year that the Department of Labor underwent a notable reorganization with the purpose of effecting the coördination necessary to complete success.

Unlike the food, fuel, and transportation problems, which were solved through new administrations not connected with the Department of

Agriculture, the Bureau of Mines, or the Interstate Commerce Commission respectively, that of labor was met by new bureaus and boards which were organic parts of the existing Department of Labor. In January, 1918, that Department undertook the formulation and administration of a national war labor policy. Shortly afterwards delegates of the National Industrial Conference Board and of the American Federation of Labor, representing capital and labor, worked out a unanimous report upon the principles to be followed in labor adjustment. To enforce these recommendations the President, on April 9, 1918, appointed a National War Labor Board, which until November sat as a court of final appeal in labor disputes. An index of the importance of the Board was given by the choice of ex-President Taft as one of its chairmen. A month later, a War Labor Policies Board was added to the system to lay down general rules for the use of the War Labor Board in the rendering of its judgments.

Not merely enthusiasm and brains enabled America to make the extraordinary efforts demanded by the exigencies of war. Behind every line of activity lay the need of money; and the raising of money in amounts so large that they passed the comprehension of the average citizen, forms one of the most romantic stories of the war. It is the story of the enthusiastic coöperation of rich and poor: Wall Street and the humblest foreign immigrants gave of their utmost in the attempt to provide the all-important funds for America and her associates in the war. Citizens accepted the weight of income and excess profit taxes far heavier than any American had previously dreamed of. They were asked in addition to buy government bonds to a total of fourteen billions, and they responded by oversubscribing this amount by nearly five billions. Of the funds needed for financing the war, the Government planned to raise about a third by taxation, and the remainder by the sale of bonds and certificates maturing in from five to thirty years. It would have proved the financial statesmanship of McAdoo had he dared to raise a larger proportion by taxation; for thus much of the inflation which inevitably resulted from the bond issues might have been avoided. But the Government feared alike for its popularity and for the immediate effect upon business, which could not safely be discouraged. As it was, the excess profit taxes aroused great complaint. The amount raised in direct taxation represented a larger proportion of the war budget than any foreign nation had been able to secure from tax revenues.

In seeking to sell its bonds the Government, rather against its will, was compelled to rely largely upon the capitalists. The large popular subscriptions would have been impossible but for the assistance and enthusiasm shown by the banks in the selling campaign. Wall Street and the bankers of the country were well prepared and responded with all their strength, a response which deserves the greater credit when we remember the lack of sympathy which had existed between financial circles and President Wilson's Administration. Largely under banking auspices the greatest selling campaign on record was inaugurated. Bonds were placed on sale at street corners, in theaters, and restaurants; disposed of by eminent operatic stars, moving-picture favorites, and wounded heroes from the front. Steeple jacks attracted crowds by their perilous antics, in order to start the bidding for subscriptions. Villages and isolated farmhouses were canvassed. The banks used their entire machinery to induce subscriptions, offering to advance the subscription price. When during the first loan campaign the rather unwise optimism of the Treasury cooled enthusiasm for a moment,

by making it appear that the loan could be floated
without effort, Wall Street took up the load. The
first loan was oversubscribed by a billion. The
success of the three loans that followed was equally
great; the fourth, coming in October, 1918, was set
for six billion dollars, the largest amount that had
ever been asked of any people, and after a three
weeks' campaign, seven billions were subscribed.
Quite as notable as the amount raised was the
progressive increase in the number of subscribers,
which ranged from four million individuals in the
first loan to more than twenty-one millions in the
fourth. Equally notable, as indicating the educative effect of the war and of the sale of these
Liberty Bonds, was the successful effort to encourage thrift. War Savings societies were instituted and children saved their pennies and nickels
to buy twenty-five cent "thrift stamps" which
might be accumulated to secure interest-bearing
savings certificates. Down to November 1, 1918,
the sale of such stamps totalled $834,253,000, with
a maturity value of more than a billion dollars.

The successful organizing of national resources
to supply military demands obviously depended,
in the last instance, upon the education of the
people to a desire for service and sacrifice. The

Liberty Loan campaigns, the appeals of Hoover, and the Fuel Administration, all were of importance in producing such morale. In addition the Council of National Defense, through the Committee on Public Information, spread pamphlets emphasizing the issues of the war and the objects for which we were fighting. At every theater and moving-picture show, in the factories during the noon hours, volunteer speakers told briefly of the needs of the Government and appealed for cooperation. These were the so-called "Four Minute Men." The most noted artists gave their talent to covering the billboards with patriotic and informative posters. Blue Devils who had fought at Verdun, captured tanks, and airplanes, were paraded in order to bring home the realities of the life and death struggle in which America was engaged. The popular response was inspiring. In the face of the national enthusiasm the much-vaunted plans of the German Government for raising civil disturbance fell to the ground. Labor was sometimes disorganized by German propaganda; destruction of property or war material was accomplished by German agents; and valuable information sometimes leaked out to the enemy. But the danger was always kept in check by the

Department of Justice and also by a far-reaching citizen organization, the American Protective League. Equally surprising was the lack of opposition to the war on the part of pacifists and socialists. It was rare to find the "sedition" for which some of them were punished, perhaps over-promptly, translated from words to actions.

The organization of the industrial resources of the nation was complicated by the same conditions that affected the purely military problems — decentralization and the emergency demands that resulted from the sudden decision to send a large expeditionary force to France. The various organizing boards were so many individual solutions for individual problems. At the beginning of the war the Council of National Defense represented the only attempt at a central business organization, and as time went on the importance and the influence of the Council diminished. The effects of decentralization became painfully apparent during the bitter cold of the winter months, when the fuel, transportation, and food crises combined to threaten almost complete paralysis of the economic and military mobilization.

The distrust and discouragement that followed

brought forth furious attacks upon the President's war policies, led not merely by Roosevelt and Republican enemies of the Administration, but by Democratic Senators. The root of the whole difficulty, they contended, lay in the fact that Wilson had no policy. They demanded practically the abdication of the presidential control of military affairs, either through the creation of a Ministry of Munitions or of a War Cabinet. In either case Congress would control the situation through its definition of the powers of the new organization and the appointment of its personnel.

President Wilson utilized the revolt to secure the complete centralization toward which he had been aiming. He fought the new proposals on the ground that they merely introduced new machinery to complicate the war organization, and he insisted that true policy demanded rather an increase in the efficiency of existing machinery. If the General Staff and the War Industries Board were given power to supervise and execute as well as to plan, the country would have the machinery at hand capable of forming a central organization, which could determine in the first place what was wanted and where, and in the second place how it could be supplied. All that was necessary was to give the President a free hand to effect any transfer of organization, funds, or functions in any of the existing departments of government, without being compelled to apply to Congress in each case.

The struggle between Wilson and his opponents was sharp, but the President carried the day. He exerted to the full his influence on Congress and utilized skillfully the argument that at this moment of crisis a swapping of horses might easily prove fatal. Opposing Congressmen drew back at the thought of shouldering the responsibility which they knew the President would throw upon them if he were defeated. On May 20, 1918, the Overman Act became law, giving to the President the blanket powers which he demanded and which he immediately used to centralize the military and industrial organization. Bureau chiefs were bitter in their disapproval; the National Guard grumbled, even as it fought its best battles in France; politicians saw their chance of influencing military affairs disappear; business men complained of the economic dictatorship thus secured by the President. But Mr. Wilson was at last in a position to effect that which seemed to him of greatest importance — the concentration of responsibility and authority.

Upon the shoulders of the President, accordingly, must rest in the last instance the major portion of the blame and the credit to be distributed for the mistakes and the achievements of the military and economic organization. He took no part in the working out of details. Once the development of any committee of organization had been started, he left the control of it entirely to those who had been placed in charge. But he would have been untrue to his nature if he had not at all times been determined to keep the reins of supreme control in his own hands. His opponents insisted that the organization was formed in spite of him. It is probable that he did not himself perceive the crying need for centralization so clearly in 1917 as he did in 1918; and the protests of his political opponents doubtless brought the realization of its necessity more definitely home to him. But there is no evidence to indicate that the process of centralization was forced upon him against his will and much to show that he sought always that concentration of responsibility and power which he insisted upon in politics. The task was herculean; ironically enough it was facilitated by the revolt against his war policies which resulted in the Senate investigation and the Overman Act.

His tactics were by no means above reproach, and his entire policy nearly went on the rocks in the winter of 1917 because of his inability to treat successfully with the Senate and with Republican Congressmen.

When all is said, however, the organization that was developed during the last six months of the war transported and maintained in Europe more than a million and a half American soldiers; at home it maintained two millions more, ready to sail at the earliest opportunity; and it was prepared to raise and equip an army of five and a half millions by June 30, 1920. The process had been slow and the results were not apparent for many months. Furthermore, because of the intensity of the danger and the absolute need of victory, cherished traditions were sacrificed and steps taken which were to cost much later on; for the price of these achievements was inevitable reaction and social unrest. But with all the mistakes and all the cost, the fact still remains that the most gigantic transformation of history — the transformation of an unmilitary and peace-loving nation of ninety million souls into a belligerent power — was successfully accomplished.

CHAPTER VIII

THE FIGHTING FRONT

THE encouragement given to the Allies by the entrance of the United States into the war injected a temporary ray of brightness into the situation abroad, but with the realization that long months must elapse before American aid could prove effective, came deep disappointment. The spring of 1917 did not bring the expected success to the French and British on the western front; and the summer and autumn carried intense discouragement. Hindenburg, early in the spring, executed a skillful retreat on the Somme front, which gave to the Allies the territory to which their previous capture of Peronne and Bapaume entitled them. But the Germans, losing some square miles, saved their troops and supplies. British attacks on the north gained little ground at terrible cost. The French offensive, planned by Nivelle, which was designed to break the German line, had to be given up after bloody checks. There was mutiny in the French armies and the morale of the civilian population sank.

The hopes that had been aroused by the Russian revolution were seen to be deceptive; instead of a national movement directed towards a more active struggle against Germany, it now appeared in its true colors as a demand for peace and land above everything. The Brusilov attack, which the Allies insisted upon, proved to be a flash in the pan and ended with the complete military demoralization of Russian armies. The collapse of the Italian forces at Caporetto followed. Italy was not merely unable to distract the attention of the Central Powers by a determined offensive against Austria, but she threatened to become a liability; no one knew how many French divisions might have to be diverted to aid in the defense of the new Piave front. General Byng's break of the German lines at Cambrai was more than offset by the equally brilliant German counter-attack. And every day the submarine was taking its toll of Allied shipping.

Following the Italian débâcle, the Bolshevik revolution of November indicated that Russia would wholly withdraw and that that great potential source of man-power for the Allies could no longer be counted upon. Allied leaders realized that Germany would be able to transfer large numbers of troops to the western front, and became seriously alarmed. "The Allies are very weak," cabled General Pershing, on the 2d of December, "and we must come to their relief this year, 1918. The year after may be too late. It is very doubtful if they can hold on until 1919 unless we give them a lot of support this year." Showing that the schedule of troop shipments would be inadequate and complaining that the actual shipments were not even being kept up to programme, Pershing insisted upon the importance of the most strenuous efforts to secure extra tonnage, which alone would make it possible for the American army to take a proper share in the military operations of 1918.

The serious representations of General Pershing were reinforced by Colonel House when he returned from abroad on the 15th of December. For six weeks he had been in conference, as head of a war mission, with the Allied political and military leaders, who now realized the necessity of unity of plan. Because of his personal intimacy with French and British statesmen and his acknowledged skill in negotiations, House had done much to bring about Allied harmony and to pave the way for a supreme military command. Like Pershing, he was convinced of the danger threatening the Allies, and from the moment of his return began the speeding-up process, which was to result in the presence of a large American force on the battle front at the moment of crisis in the early summer of 1918.

Tonnage was obviously the vital factor upon which effective military assistance depended. The United States had the men, although they were not completely trained, but the apparent impossibility of transporting them formed the great obstacle. The problem could not have been solved without the assistance of the Allies. With the threat of the German drive, and especially after the first German victories of 1918, they began to appreciate the necessity of sacrificing everything to the tonnage necessary to transport American soldiers to France. After long hesitation they agreed to a pooling of Allied tonnage for this purpose. Most of the Allied ships ultimately furnished the United States were provided by the British, whose transports carried a million American troops to France. French and Italian boats transported 112,000; our own transports, 927,000.

Thus by relying largely upon the shipping assistance of our associates in the war we were able to respond to the demands of General Pershing and, later, Marshal Foch. And thus came about the extraordinary development of our military programme from the thirty to the eighty and one hundred division plans, which resulted in tremendous confusion, but which also ultimately ensured Allied victory in 1918. Until the end of the year 1917, we had put into France only 195,000 troops, including 7500 marines, an average of about 28,000 a month. From December to February the average rose to 48,000; from March to May it was 149,000; and from June to August it was 290,000 men a month. During the four months from May to August inclusive, 1,117,000 American troops were transported to France.

Altogether about two million Americans were sent to France, without the loss of a single man while under the escort of United States vessels. No navy troop transports were torpedoed on eastbound trips although three were sunk on the return trip with loss of 138 lives. To the American and British navies must go the credit for carrying through this stupendous feat, and in the work of assuring the safety of the troop transports the navy of the United States may claim recognition for the larger share, since 82 per cent of the escorts furnished were American cruisers and destroyers. It was a nerve-racking and tantalizing experience — the troop ships sailing in echelon formation, preceded, followed, and flanked by destroyers; at night every glimmer of light eclipsed, the ships speeding ahead in perfect blackness, each inch of the sea swept by watchful eyes to discover the telltale ripple of a periscope or the trail of a torpedo, gun crews on the alert, depth bombs ready. Nor was the crossing anything like a vacation yachting cruise for the doughboys transported, packed as they were like sardines two and three decks below the waterline, brought up in shifts to catch a brief taste of fresh air, assailed at once by homesickness, seasickness, and fears of drowning like rats in a trap.

The work of the navy was far more extensive, moreover, than the safe convoying of troop ships, important though that was. The very first contingent of American overseas fighting forces was made up of two flotillas of destroyers, which upon the declaration of war had been sent to Queenstown where they were placed under the command of Admiral William S. Sims. Their main function was to hunt submarines, which, since the decree of the 1st of February, had succeeded in committing frightful ravages upon Allied commerce and seriously threatened to starve the British Isles. Admiral Sims was two years older than Pershing and as typical a sailor as the former was soldier. With his bluff and genial, yet dignified, manner, his rubicund complexion, closely-trimmed white beard, and piercing eyes, no one could have mistaken his calling. Free of speech, frank in praise and criticism, abounding in indiscretions, he possessed the capacity to make the warmest friends and enemies. He was an ardent admirer of the British, rejoiced in fighting with them, and ashamed that our Navy Department was unwilling to send more adequate and immediate assistance to their fleet. Sims's international reputation as an expert in naval affairs was of long standing. Naval officers in every country of Europe knew of him as the inventor of a system of fire control which had been adopted by the great navies of the world, and it was largely because of his studies and devices that the extraordinary records of the American fleets at target practice had been secured. The British naval officers reciprocated Sims's admiration for them, and, according to popular belief, it was at their special request that he had been sent to command our overseas naval forces. No one else could have obtained such effective coöperation between the British and American fleets.

While at first the major portion of the American fleet was retained in home waters for the protection of American coasts and ports, a policy which aroused the stinging criticism of Admiral Sims, gradually the fleet added strength to the Allied navies in their patrol of European coasts and the bottling-up of the German high seas fleet. Destroyer bases were maintained at Queenstown, Brest, and Gibraltar, from which were dispatched constant patrols. Individual destroyers, during the first year of service overseas, steamed a total of 60,000 miles. Their crews were on the watch in the dirtiest weather, unable to sleep, tossed and battered by the incessant rolling, without warm food, facing the constant peril of being swept overboard and knowing that their boat could not stop to pick them up. American submarine-chasers and converted yachts, mine-sweepers on their beneficent and hazardous duty, were equally active. Naval aviators coöperated with the British to patrol the coasts in search of submarines. Late in 1917, six battleships were sent to join the British Grand Fleet, which was watching for the Germans in the North Sea, thus constituting about twelve per cent of the guarding naval force. More important, perhaps, was the American plan for laying a mine barrage from the Scotch coast across to Norwegian waters. The Ordnance Bureau of the navy, despite the discouragement of British experts, manufactured the mines, 100,000 of them, and shipped them abroad in parts ready for final assembling. The American navy was responsible for eighty per cent of the laying of the barrage, which when finished was 245 miles long and twenty miles wide. The complete story of the achievements of the navy cannot now be told in detail. It was not always inspiring, for numerous mistakes were made. Confusion of counsels in the Naval Board left one important bombing squadron so bereft of supplies that after an expenditure of four millions only two bombs were dropped in the entire course of its operations. But there are also to be remembered the unheralded stories of heroism and skill, such as the dash of the submarine-chasers and destroyers through the mine fields at Durazzo, and the work of our naval guns in the attack on Zeebrugge.

The armies, safely brought to France, were meanwhile undergoing the essential intensive training, and the task of organizing the service of supply was being undertaken. The training given in the United States before sailing had been in the ordinary forms of drill and tactics; now it was necessary that there should be greater specialization. Numerous schools for the training of officers were established. For the troops the plan for training allowed, according to the intent of General Pershing, "a division one month for acclimatization and instruction in small units from battalions down, a second month in quiet trench sectors by battalion, and a third month after it came out of the trenches when it should be trained as a complete division in war of movement."[1] The entire process of training was a compromise between speed and efficiency. During the latter months of the war many of the American troops were put on the battle-line when they were by no means sufficiently trained. Certain draft units were transported and thrown up to the front after experience of a most superficial character; there are instances of men going into action without knowing how to load their rifles or adjust their gas masks properly. But on the whole the training given was surprisingly

[1] This plan could not be fulfilled for troops coming to France in 1918, because of lack of time.

effective in view of the speed with which it was accomplished. American skill with the rifle won the envy of foreign officers, and the value of American troops in open warfare was soon to be acknowledged by the Germans.

The same sort of centralization sought by Wilson in America obviously became necessary in France with the expanding plans for an enormous army. In February, 1918, the Service of Supply was organized. With its headquarters at Tours, the S. O. S. was responsible for securing, organizing, and distributing all the food, equipment, building materials, and other necessities demanded by the expeditionary force. In order to provide for the quantities of essential supplies and to avoid the congestion of the chief ports of France, certain ports were especially allotted to our army, of which the most important were St. Nazaire, Bordeaux, and Brest. The first, a somnolent fishing village, was transformed by the energy of American engineers into a first-class port with enormous docks, warehouses, and supply depots; Brest rose in the space of twelve months from the rank of a second-class port to one that matched Hamburg in the extent of its shipping. In all, more than a dozen ports were used by the Americans and in each extensive improvements and enlargements proved necessary. At Bordeaux not more than two ships a week, of any size, could conveniently be unloaded prior to June, 1917. Eight months later, docks a mile long had been constructed, concrete platforms and electric cranes set up; within a year fourteen ships could be unloaded simultaneously, the rate of speed being determined only by the number of stevedores. For unloading purposes regiments of negroes were stationed at each port.

A few miles back from the coast were the base depots where the materials were stored as they came from the ships. Thence distribution was made to the intermediate depots in the cities of supply, and finally to the depots immediately behind the fighting front. All these depots involved enormous building operations; at first the lumber was shipped, but later, American lumber jacks were brought over to cut French forests. At one supply depot three hundred buildings were put up, covering an area of six square miles, operated by 20,000 men, and holding in storage a hundred million dollars' worth of supplies. For distribution purposes it proved necessary for American engineers to take over the construction and maintenance of communications. At first American engines and cars were operated under French supervision; but ultimately many miles of French railroads were taken over bodily by the American army and many more built by American engineers. More than 400 miles of inland waterways were also used by American armies. This transportation system was operated by American experts of all grades from brakemen to railroad presidents, numbering altogether more than 70,000.

In order to meet the difficulty of securing tonnage for supplies and to avoid competition with the Allies, a General Purchasing Board was created for the coördination of all purchases. Agents of this board were stationed in the Allied countries, in Switzerland, Holland, and Spain, who reconnoitered resources, analyzed requirements, issued forecasts of supplies, supervised the claims of foreign governments on American raw materials, and procured civilian manual labor. Following the establishment of the supreme interallied command, the Interallied Board of Supplies was organized in the summer of 1918, with the American purchasing agent as a member. Other activities of the S. O. S., too numerous to recount in detail, included such important tasks as the reclassification of personnel, the installation and operation of a general service of telephone and telegraph communication, with 115,500 kilometers of lines, and the renting and requisitioning of the land and buildings needed by the armies. It was a gigantic business undertaking, organized at top speed, involving tremendous expenditure. Its success would have been impossible without the coöperation of hundreds of men of business, who found in it a sphere of service which enabled the army to utilize the proverbial American genius for meeting large problems of economic organization. At the time of the armistice the S. O. S. reached a numerical strength in personnel of 668,000, including 23,000 civilian employees.

From the first, Pershing had been determined that the American Expeditionary Force should ultimately operate as an independent unit, although in close coöperation with the Allies. During the autumn of 1917 the disasters in Italy and the military demoralization of Russia had led to the formation of the Supreme Military Council of the Allies, upon which the United States was represented by General Tasker Bliss, whose rough visage and gruff manner gave little indication of his wide interests. Few suspected that this soldierly character took secret pleasure in the reading of Latin poets. The coördination that resulted from the creation of the Supreme Council, however, proved insufficient to meet the crisis of the spring of 1918.

On the 21st of March, the Germans attacked in overwhelming force the southern extremity of the British lines, near where they joined the French, and disastrously defeated General Gough's army. The break-through was clean and the advance made by the endless waves of German shock-troops appalling. Within eight days the enemy had swept forward to a depth of fifty-six kilometers, threatening the capture of Amiens and the separation of the French and British. As the initial momentum of the onslaught was lost, the Allied line was re-formed with the help of French reserves under Fayolle. But the Allies had been and still were close to disaster. Complete unity of command was essential. It was plain also, in the words of Pershing's report, that because of the inroads made upon British and French reserves, "defeat stared them in the face unless the new American troops should prove more immediately available than even the most optimistic had dared to hope." The first necessity was satisfied early in April. The extremity of the danger reinforced the demand long made by the French, and supported by President Wilson through Colonel House, that a generalissimo be appointed. The British finally sank their objection, and on the 28th of March it was agreed that General Ferdinand Foch should be made commander-in-chief of all the Allied armies with the powers necessary for the strategic direction of all military operations. The decision was ratified on the 3d and approved by President Wilson on the 16th of April.

General Foch had long been recognized as an eminent student of strategy, and he had proved his practical capacity in 1914 and later. It was he who commanded the French army that broke the German line at the marshes of St. Gond, in the battle of the Marne, thus assuring victory to Joffre, and he had later in the year secured fresh laurels in the first battle of the Yser. At the moment of extreme danger to Italy, after Caporetto, in 1917, he had been chosen to command the assisting force sent down by the French. Unsentimental and unswayed by political factors, he was temperamentally and intellectually the ideal man for the post of supreme Allied commander; he was furthermore supported by the capacity of General Pétain, the French commander-in-chief, and by a remarkable group of army commanders, among whom Fayolle, Mangin, and Gouraud were to win particular fame. But he lacked troops, the Germans disposing of 200 divisions as against 162 Allied divisions.

Hence the hurry call sent to America and hence the heavy sacrifice now forced upon Pershing. Much against his will and only as a result of extreme pressure, the American commander-in-chief agreed to a temporary continuance of the brigading of American troops with the British and the French. He had felt all along that "there was every reason why we could not allow them to be scattered among our Allies, even by divisions, much less as replacements, except by pressure of pure necessity." He disliked the emphasis placed by the Allies upon training for trench warfare; he feared the effect of the lack of homogeneity which would render the mixed divisions "difficult to maneuver and almost certain to break up under the stress of defeat," and he believed that the creation of independent American armies "would be a severe blow to German morale." When the pinch of necessity came, however, Pershing sank his objections to amalgamation and, to his credit, agreed with a *beau geste* and fine phrase which concealed the differences between the Allied chiefs and won the heartiest sympathy from France and England. The principle of an independent American force, however, Pershing insisted upon, and he made clear that the amalgamation of our troops with the French and British was merely a temporary expedient.

Immediately after the stabilization of the battle-line near Amiens, the Germans began their second great drive, this time against the British along the Lys, in Flanders. The initial success of the attack, which began on the 9th of April, was undeniable, and Sir Douglas Haig himself admitted the danger of the moment: "Every position must be held to the last man. There must be no retirement. With our backs to the wall and believing in the justice of our cause, each one of us must fight to the end. The safety of our homes and the freedom of mankind depend alike upon the conduct of each one of us at this critical moment." The value of Allied unity of command now became apparent, for heavy French reinforcements were brought up in time to help stave off the German drive on the Channel Ports.

But still the demand went up for more men and ships. "Scrap before shipping every pound that takes tonnage and is not necessary to the killing of Germans," wrote a French military authority

"Send the most infantry by the shortest route to the hottest corner. No matter what flag they fight under, so long as it is an Allied flag." On the 27th of May the Germans caught Foch by surprise and launched a violent attack on the Chemin des Dames, between Soissons and Berry-au-Bac. This formed the third phase of their great offensive. In four days they pushed before them the tired French divisions, sent into that sector to recuperate, a distance of fifty kilometers and reached the Marne. Again, as in 1914, Paris began to empty, fearful of capture. A statement sent to Wilson on the 2d of June and signed by Clemenceau, Lloyd George, and Orlando, read as follows: "There is great danger of the war being lost unless the numerical inferiority of the Allies can be remedied as rapidly as possible by the advent of American troops. . . . We are satisfied that General Foch . . . is not over-estimating the needs of the case." Such was the peril of the Allies. But in the month of May 245,000 Americans had been landed, and in the following month there were to be 278,000 more.

Previous to June, 1918, the participation of American troops in military operations had been of comparative unimportance and less for tactical purposes than as a part of their training. In

October, 1917, the First Division had been sent into trenches on the quiet Lorraine front and had engaged in raids and counter-raids. Three other divisions, the Second, the Forty-second, or "Rainbow," and the Twenty-sixth from New England, followed, and by March, 1918, they were all described by Pershing as "equal to any demands of battle action." On the 29th of April, the last-named division was engaged in something more serious than a mere raid at Seicheprey, near St. Mihiel; the number of prisoners lost indicated lack of experience, but the vigor of the American counter-attack proved definitely the will to fight. That belligerent spirit was equally displayed by various engineering units which, during the break of General Gough's army before the German assault of March, near St. Quentin, had dropped their tools, seized rifles, and, hastily organizing to cover the retreat, had secured valuable respite for various fleeing units.

More important yet, because of the moral effect achieved, was the engagement at Cantigny near Montdidier, on the 28th of May. The Americans launched their attack with skill as well as dash, and stood firm against the violence of the German reaction; this they met without assistance from the

French, who had been called to oppose the German advance on the Marne. Pershing spoke of the "desperate efforts" of the enemy at Cantigny, "determined at all costs to counteract the most excellent effect the American success had produced." For three days guns of all calibers were vainly concentrated upon the new positions. Coming at the moment of extreme discouragement, Cantigny was of an importance entirely out of proportion to the numbers involved. For months France had been awaiting American assistance. A year before the French had seen Pershing and the first few doughboys, but the long delay had caused them to lose the confidence which that sight had aroused. Now suddenly came the news that the Americans were arriving in tremendous numbers and from Cantigny, north and south along the lines, spread the report: "These men will fight."

Four days later at Château-Thierry,[1] Americans proved not merely the moral but the practical value of their assistance. The German drive of the 27th of May, beginning on the Chemin des Dames, had pushed south to the Marne and westward

[1] The reader should distinguish the defensive operations at Château-Thierry, on the 1st of June, from the attack launched from this sector in July. Both are known as the battle of Château-Thierry.

towards Meaux. The French falling back in haste had maintained their lines intact, but were pessimistic as to the possibility of stopping the enemy advance. On the 31st of May, German vanguard units entered Château-Thierry, crossed the river, and planned to secure the bridges. At this moment American machine gunners of the Third Division came up with a battalion of French colonials in support, drove the Germans back to the north bank, covered the retreat of the French forces across the Marne, on the following day, and gave time to blow up the bridges. On the same day, the 1st of June, northwest of Château-Thierry, the Second Division came into line to support the wearied French, and as the latter came filtering back and through, soon found itself meeting direct German assaults. Stretching across the road to Paris, with the French too weak to make a stand, it blocked the German advance. Even so, the danger was not entirely parried, since the enemy held strong positions from Vaux northwest to Veuilly, which, when German reinforcements came up, would enable them to deliver deadly assaults. Those positions had to be taken. From the 6th to the 11th of June, American troops, among them marine regiments, struck viciously, concentrating against the railroad embankment at Bouresches and the hill of Belleau Woods. The stiffness of the German defense, maintained by their best troops, was overcome by fearless rushing of machine-gun nests, ruthless mopping-up of isolated stragglers, and a final clearing of the Woods by heavy artillery fire. On the 18th of June the Americans took the approaches to Torcy and on the 1st of July the village of Vaux. If the attack on Belleau Woods proved their courage, the capture of Vaux vindicated their skill, for losses were negligible.

The Allied line was now in a position to contest actively any deepening of the Marne salient to the west, and American troops had so clearly proved their quality that Pershing could with justice demand a radical revision of the Allied opinion that American soldiers were fit only for the defense. His confidence in their fighting capacity was soon further put to the test and vindicated. On the 15th of July the Germans opened the fourth and last of their great drives, with tremendous artillery fire from Rheims to the Marne. They hoped to capture the former, swing far to the south and west, and, if they failed to take Paris, at least to draw sufficient troops from Flanders and Picardy as to assure a successful drive on Amiens and the Channel

Ports. For the first time, however, the element of surprise in their attack was lacking. At the eastern end of the battle-line General Gouraud, with whom were fighting the Forty-second Division and four colored regiments, warned of the moment of attack, withdrew his front lines and permitted the Germans to shell empty trenches; all important positions he held firmly. On the Marne, east of Château-Thierry, the enemy succeeded in crossing the river in the early morning. At various points the American line was compelled to yield, although one of the American regiments stood its ground while on either flank the Germans, who had gained a footing on the south bank, pressed forward; it was, according to Pershing's report, "one of the most brilliant pages in our military annals." At noon, heedless of the warning given by the French commander, American reinforcements launched a strong counter-attack and drove the enemy back to the river; on the next morning no Germans were to be found on the south bank in front of the American troops. During the next two days German efforts to press forward were unrelaxing but in vain, and on the 18th of July, Foch launched his counter-offensive.

The inherent weakness of the Marne salient from

the German point of view and the opportunity which it offered the Allied command had not been forgotten by the generalissimo. Foch waited until the enemy had spent his strength in the attacks around Rheims and on the Marne, then struck fiercely between Soissons and Château-Thierry. The spearhead of the main drive was composed of the First and Second American Divisions, immediately to the south of Soissons, who were operating under Mangin with the First French Moroccan Division between them. Straightway, without the orthodox preliminary artillery fire, a deep thrust was made against the western side of the salient; near Soissons, despite fierce resistance, advances of from eight to ten kilometers and large numbers of prisoners were reported in the first twenty-four hours. "Due to the magnificent dash and powers displayed on the field of Soissons by our First and Second Divisions," said Pershing, "the tide of war was definitely turned in favor of the Allies." Further to the south, the Fourth and Twenty-sixth Divisions crossed the road running from Château-Thierry to Soissons, pushing east; while from the southern bank of the Marne, the Third Division pushed north across the river. It was obvious to the Germans that retreat from the perilous salient must proceed at once, especially as Franco-British counter-attacks on the eastern side threatened to close it at the neck and cut the main line of German withdrawal. The retreat was executed with great skill and valor. While holding on the sides, the enemy forces were slowly pulled back from the apex, striving to win time to save artillery, although they must perforce lose or destroy great quantities of ammunition. Against the retreating foe fresh American divisions were hurled. On the 25th of July the Forty-second division relieved the Twenty-sixth, advancing toward the Vesle, with elements of the Twenty-eighth, until relieved on August 3d, by the Fourth Division. Farther east the Thirty-second had relieved the Third. The Americans had to face withering fire from machine-gun nests and fight hand to hand in the crumbled streets of the Champagne villages. Here were carried on some of the fiercest conflicts of American military history. Finally on the 6th of August the Germans reached the line of the Vesle, their retreat secured, although their losses had been terrific. But the pause was only momentary. Before they could bring up replacements, the British launched their great drive south of the Somme, the American Twenty-eighth, Thirty-second, and

Seventy-seventh divisions crossed the Vesle pushing the Germans before them, and there began what Ludendorff in his memoirs calls "the last phase."

Pershing had not lost sight of his original object, which was to assemble the American divisions into a separate army. After the victories of July, which wiped out the Marne salient, and those of August, which put the enemy definitely on the defensive, he felt that "the emergency which had justified the dispersion of our divisions had passed." Soon after the successful British attack, south of Amiens, he overcame the objections of Foch and concluded arrangements for the organization of this army, which was to operate in the Lorraine sector.[1] It contained 600,000 men, fourteen American divisions and two French. On the 30th of August the sector was established and preparations made for the offensive, the first step in which was to be the wiping out of the St. Mihiel salient. This salient had existed since 1914, when the Germans, failing to storm the scarp protecting Verdun on the east, had driven a wedge across the lower heights to the south. The elimination of this wedge would have

[1] Allied opposition to an American army was so strong as to bring threats of an appeal to Wilson. The President steadfastly supported Pershing.

great moral effect; it would free the Paris-Nancy railway from artillery fire; and would assure Pershing an excellent base for attack against the Metz-Sedan railway system and the Briey iron basin. The German positions were naturally strong and had withstood violent French attacks in 1915. But there was only one effective line of retreat and the enemy, if he persisted in holding the apex of the salient, risked losing his entire defending force, should the sides be pressed in from the south and west.

On the 12th of September the attack was launched. It was originally planned for the 15th, but word was brought that the Germans were about to retire at a rate which would have left none of them in the salient by that date. Hence the attack was advanced by three days. The attempted withdrawal secured the retreat of the German main force, but they were unable to save their rear guard. After four hours of vigorous artillery preparation, with the largest assemblage of aviation ever engaged in a single operation (mainly British and French) and with American heavy guns throwing into confusion all rail movements behind the German lines, the advancing Americans immediately overwhelmed all of the enemy that attempted to hold their ground. By the afternoon of the second day the salient was extinguished, 16,000 prisoners were taken, 443 guns and large stores of supplies captured. American casualties totaled less than 7000. The effects of the victory were incalculable. Apart from the material results, hope of which had motivated the attack, the moral influence of the battle of St. Mihiel in the making of American armies and the discouragement of the German High Command was of the first importance. "An American army was an accomplished fact," wrote Pershing, "and the enemy had felt its power. No form of propaganda could overcome the depressing effect on the morale of the enemy of this demonstration of our ability to organize a large American force and drive it successfully through his defense. It gave our troops implicit confidence in their superiority and raised their morale to the highest pitch. For the first time wire entanglements ceased to be regarded as impassable barriers and open-warfare training, which had been so urgently insisted upon, proved to be the correct doctrine."

The victory of St. Mihiel was merely the necessary prelude to greater things. During the first week of September the Allied command decided that the general offensive movement of their armies should be pressed as rapidly as possible, converging upon the main line of German retreat through Mezières and Sedan. The British were to pursue the attack in the direction of Cambrai, the center of the French armies, west of Rheims, was to drive the enemy beyond the Aisne, while the Americans were to attack through the Argonne and on both sides of the Meuse, aiming for Sedan. Pershing was given his choice of the Champagne or Argonne sectors, and chose the latter, which was the more difficult, insisting that no other Allied troops possessed the offensive spirit which would be necessary for success. In the meantime a new American army was to be organized, to operate south of Verdun and against Metz, in the spring of 1919; in fact this was designed to be the chief American effort. As matters turned out this second American army was ready to make its offensive early in November, but in September none of the Allied chiefs expressed the opinion that the final victory could be achieved in 1918. Such were the difficulties of terrain in the Argonne advance that the French did not believe that the attack could be pushed much beyond Montfaucon, between the forest and the Meuse, before winter forced a cessation of active operations.

The defensive importance of the Argonne for the Germans could hardly be overestimated, for if the railway line running through Sedan and Mezières were severed, they would be cut in two by the Ardennes and would be unable to withdraw from France the bulk of their forces, which, left without supplies, would suffer inevitable disaster. As a consequence the Argonne had been strengthened by elaborate fortifications which, taken in conjunction with the natural terrain, densely wooded, covered with rugged heights, and marked by ridges running east and west, made it apparently impregnable. The dense undergrowth, the bowlders, and the ravines offered ideal spots for machine-gun nests. The Germans had the exact range of each important position.

But Pershing's confidence in the offensive valor of the Americans was amply justified. On the morning of the 26th of September the initial attack was delivered, the main force of the blow falling east of the forest, where the natural strength of the enemy positions was less formidable. By noon of the second day Montfaucon was captured, and by the 29th all the immediate objectives of the attack were secured. Losses were heavy, staff work was frequently open to severe criticism, communications were broken at times, the infantry had not always received adequate artillery support, but the success of the drive was undeniable. Before the American troops, however, still lay two more lines of defense, the Freya and Kriemhilde, and the Germans were bringing up their best divisions. On the 4th of October the attack was renewed, in coöperation with the French under Gouraud to the west of the forest who pressed forward actively; a week's more bitter fighting saw the Argonne itself cleared of the enemy. Hard struggles ensued, particularly around Grandpré, which was taken and retaken, while on the east of the Meuse the enemy was pushed back. By the end of the month the Kriemhilde line had been broken and the great railway artery was threatened. On the 1st of November the third phase of the great advance began. The desperate efforts of the Germans to hold were never relaxed, but by the evening of that day the American troops broke through their last defense and forced rapid retreat. Motor trucks were hurriedly brought up for the pursuit, and by the fifth the enemy's withdrawal became general. Two days later Americans held the heights which dominated Sedan, the strategic goal, and the German line of communications was as good as severed.

The converging offensive planned by Foch had succeeded. At Cambrai, Le Câtelet, and St. Quentin, the British, with whom were operating four American divisions (the Twenty-seventh, Thirtieth, Thirty-seventh, and Ninety-first), had broken the Hindenburg line; the French had pushed the Germans back from Laon, north of the Aisne, and with the British were driving them into the narrow neck of the bottle; and now the French and Americans, by their Argonne-Meuse advance had closed the neck. The enemy faced an appalling disaster. A few weeks, if not days, of continued fighting meant the most striking military débâcle of history. Germany's allies had fallen from her. Turkey, Bulgaria, and Austria-Hungary had sued for peace and agreed to cease fighting on what amounted to terms of unconditional surrender. At home, the German Government faced revolution; the Kaiser was about to abdicate and flee. On the 6th of November, the Berlin Government begged for an immediate armistice and five days later agreed to the stringent terms which the Allies presented. On the 11th of November, at eleven in the morning, firing ceased. Until the last second the battle raged with a useless intensity dictated by stern military tradition; then perfect quiet on the battle front.

At the present moment we lack the perspective, perhaps, to evaluate exactly the share of credit which the American Expeditionary Force deserves for the Allied military victory of 1918. Previous to June the military contribution of the United States had no material effects. The defense of Château-Thierry at the beginning of the month and the operations there and at Belleau Woods had, however, important practical as well as moral effects. The fighting was of a purely local character, but it came at a critical moment and at a critical spot. It was a crisis when the importance of standing firm could not be overestimated, and the defensive capacity of the French had been seriously weakened. The advance of American divisions with the French in the clearing of the Marne sector was of the first military importance. The Americans were better qualified than any European troops, at that stage of the war, to carry through offensive operations. They were fearless not merely because of natural hardihood, but through ignorance of danger; they were fresh and undefeated, physically and morally capable of undergoing the gruelling punishment delivered by the rearguards of the retreating Germans; their training had been primarily for open warfare. The same qualities were essential for the arduous and deadly task of breaking the German line in the Argonne, which was the finishing blow on the western battlefields.

The defects of the American armies have been emphasized by European experts. They point especially to the faulty staff-work, apparent in the Argonne particularly, which resulted in heavy losses. Staff-officers in numerous instances seem to have been ill-trained and at times positively unequal to the exigencies of the campaign. Mistakes in selection account for this to some degree, for men were appointed who were not equipped temperamentally or intellectually for the positions given them. Equally frequent were mistakes in the distribution of staff-officers. It is a notable fact, however, that such mistakes resulted from inexperience and ignorance and not from the intrusion of politics. President Wilson guaranteed to General Pershing complete immunity from the pleas of politicians and in no war fought by the United States have political factors played a rôle of such insignificance.

Finally, and aside from the fighting qualities of the rank and file and certain defects of the higher command, the Americans represented numbers; and without the tremendous numerical force transported to Europe in the spring and summer, the plans of Foch could not have been completed. We have the testimony of the Allied chiefs in June that without American man-power they faced defeat. It is equally obvious that without the 1,390,000 American troops which, by November, had appeared on the fighting line, the autumn of 1918 would not have witnessed the military triumph of the Allies.

CHAPTER IX

THE PATH TO PEACE

THE armistice of November 11, 1918, resulted directly from the military defeat of German armies in France, following upon the collapse of Turkey, Bulgaria, and Austria-Hungary. But there were many circumstances other than military that led to Germany's downfall, and by no means of least importance were the moral issues so constantly stressed by Wilson. His speeches had been carefully distributed through the Central Empires; they had done much to arouse the subject peoples of Austria-Hungary to revolt for their freedom, and also to weaken the morale of the German people. The value of Wilson's "verbiage drives" was questioned in this country. Abroad, his insistence upon a peace of justice was generally reckoned a vital moral force in the political movements that supplemented the victories of Marshal Foch. Jugoslavs consented to coöperate with their Italian enemies because they felt that "Wilson's justice" would guarantee a fair court for their aspirations in the Adriatic; Magyars and Austrians threw down their arms in the belief that his promise to "be as just to enemies as to friends" secured a better future than they could hope for through the continuance of the war; the leaders of the German Reichstag demanded the Kaiser's abdication in November, under the impression that Wilson had laid it down as a condition of peace.

From the time when the United States entered the war it was obvious that Wilson placed less emphasis upon defeating Germany than upon securing a just peace. Military victory meant nothing to him except as the road to peace. In his first war speeches the President, much to the irritation of many Americans, insisted that the United States was fighting the government and not the people of Germany. "We have no quarrel," he said, "with the German people. We have no feeling towards them but one of sympathy and friendship." In his Flag Day address he was careful not to attack "Germany" but only "the military masters under whom Germany is bleeding." Certain effects of this attitude were to be seen in the Reichstag revolt of July, 1917, led by that most sensitive of political weathercocks, Matthias Erzberger, which was designed to take political control out of the hands of the military clique. That crisis, however, was safely survived by Ludendorff, who remained supreme. President Wilson then returned to the attack in his reply to the Pope's peace proposals of August. "The object of this war is to deliver the free peoples of the world from the menace and the actual power of a vast military establishment controlled by an irresponsible government. . . . This power is not the German people. It is the ruthless master of the German people. . . . We cannot take the word of the present rulers of Germany as a guarantee of anything that is to endure, unless explicitly supported by such conclusive evidence of the will and purpose of the German people themseves as the other peoples of the world would be justified in accepting."

There was serpentine wisdom in these words, for their very vagueness attracted German liberals. Wilson did not demand a republic; he did not insist upon the Kaiser's abdication, for which Germany was not then prepared; all that he asked was a government responsible to the people, and more and more the Germans were demanding that themselves. Furthermore, he again laid stress upon the fact that the Germans need not fear vengeance such as the Allies had threatened. "Punitive damages, the dismemberment of empires, the establishment of selfish and exclusive economic leagues, we deem inexpedient." The appeal was fruitless in its immediate effects, for the political party leaders were still dominated by the military; but ultimately, in conjunction with a dozen other appeals, its influence acted like a subtle corrosive upon the German will to conquer.

Still less successful were the attempts to win Austria away from her ally by secret diplomatic conversations. In these neither President Wilson nor his personal adviser, Colonel House, placed great confidence. They had been undertaken by the French through Prince Sixtus of Bourbon, and in August, 1917, Major Armand of France discussed with the Austrian emissary, Revertata, possible means of bringing about peace between Austria and the Allies. Lloyd George enthusiastically approved this attempt to drive a wedge between Austria and Germany, was anxious to send Lord Reading as intermediary, and, upon the refusal of the latter to undertake the mission, actually dispatched General Smuts to Switzerland.

The Emperor Carl seemed sincerely anxious to make sacrifices for peace and was urged by liberal counselors, such as Förster and Lammasch, in whom the Allies had confidence, to meet many of the demands of his discontented Slav subjects by granting autonomy to the Czechs, Poles, and Jugoslavs. Negotiations were hampered by the belief of the Italians that immediate peace with Austria would prevent them from securing the territories they coveted; by the sullen obstinacy of the Magyars, who were jealous of their mastery over the Hungarian Slavs, and above all, as Colonel House had foreseen, by Austria's fear of Germany. In fact it was a stern ultimatum sent by Ludendorff that brought the wavering Carl back to his allegiance.

In the autumn of 1917, however, talk of peace was in the air and a definite demand for its consideration was made in a noteworthy speech by Lord Lansdowne, a Conservative leader in England. Negotiations were inaugurated between Germany and the new Bolshevik Government of Russia, and for a few weeks at the beginning of the new year the war-weary world seemed close to the possibility of a general understanding. For the first time Lloyd George outlined in specific language the main terms that would be considered by the Allies. It was President Wilson's opportunity. Careless of securing an overwhelming military victory, indeed unwilling to crush Germany, anxious to pledge the Entente to his programme in this moment of their discouragement, he formulated on January 8, 1918, his Fourteen Points, upon which he declared the final peace settlement should be based. His speech was at once an appeal to the liberals and peace-hungry of the Central Empires, a warning to the military clique in Germany then preparing to enforce degrading terms upon Russia, and a notification to the Allies that the United States could not be counted upon to fight for selfish national interests. He reiterated the principles which had actuated the United States when it entered the war: "What we demand in this war, therefore, is nothing peculiar to ourselves. It is that the world be made fit and safe to live in; and particularly that it be made safe for every peace-loving nation which, like our own, wishes to live its own life, determine its own institutions, be assured of justice and fair dealing by the other peoples of the world as against force and selfish aggression. All the peoples of the world are in effect partners in this interest, and for our own part we see very clearly that unless justice be done to others it will not be done to us."

Of the Fourteen Points into which he then divided his peace programme, the first five were general in nature. The first insisted upon open diplomacy, to begin with the approaching Peace Conference: "Open covenants of peace, openly arrived at, after which there shall be no private international understandings of any kind." Next came "absolute freedom of navigation upon the seas . . . alike in peace and in war." Then "the removal, so far as possible, of all economic barriers and the establishment of an equality of trade conditions among all the nations consenting to the peace." There followed a demand for the reduction of armaments "to the lowest point consistent with domestic safety." The fifth point called for an "impartial adjustment of all colonial claims, based upon . . . the interests of the populations concerned" as well as "the equitable claims of the government whose title is to be determined."

These generalizations were not so much God-given tables which must determine the international law of the future as they were subtle inducements to cease fighting; they were idealistic in tone, but intensely practical in purpose. They guaranteed to any Germans who wanted peace that there would be protection against British "navalism," against the threatened Allied economic boycott, as well as a chance of the return of the conquered colonies. The force of their seductiveness was proved, when, many months later, in October, 1918, defeated Germany grasped at them as a drowning man at a straw. At the same time Wilson offered to liberals the world over the hope of ending the old-style secret diplomacy, and to business men and labor the termination of the system of competitive armaments, with their economic and moral waste. No one would suggest that Wilson did not believe in the idealism of these first five points; no one should forget, however, that they were carefully drafted with the political situation of the moment definitely in view. They might be construed as a charter for future international relations, but they were designed primarily to serve as a diplomatic weapon for the present.

Each of the succeeding eight points was more special in character, and dealt with the territorial and political problems of the warring states. They provided for the evacuation and restoration of all conquered territories in Europe, including Russia, Belgium, France, and the Balkan States. The sovereignty of Belgium should be unlimited in future; the "wrong done to France by Prussia in 1871 in the matter of Alsace-Lorraine . . . should be righted"; Italian frontiers should be readjusted "along clearly recognizable lines of nationality"; the peoples of Austria-Hungary "should be accorded the freest opportunity of autonomous development"; the relations of the Balkan States should be determined "along historically established lines of allegiance and nationality"; nationalities under Turkish rule should receive opportunity for security of life and autonomous development, and the Dardanelles should be permanently opened to all nations under international guarantees; an independent Polish state should be erected to "include the territories inhabited by indisputably Polish populations, which should be assured a free and secure access to the sea."

Generally speaking these stipulations seemed to guarantee the moderate war aims of the Entente and corresponded closely to the demands made by Lloyd George; they certainly repudiated the extreme purposes attributed to German imperialists. And yet these eight points were so vague and capable of such diverse interpretation that, like the first five general points, they might prove not unattractive to liberals in Germany and Austria. France was not definitely promised Alsace-Lorraine; any hint at the dismemberment of Austria-Hungary was carefully avoided; the readjustment of Italian frontiers might mean much or little. What were "historically established lines of allegiance and nationality" in the Balkans? And if Poland were to include only populations "indisputably Polish," was it possible to assure them "free and secure access to the sea"? The political advantage in such generalities was obvious. But there was also great danger. The time might come when both belligerent camps would accept the Fourteen Points and would still be uncertain of their meaning and application. The struggle for definite interpretation would be the real test. The President's fourteenth and last point, however, was unmistakable and expressed the ideal nearest his heart: "A general association of nations must be formed under specific covenants for the purpose of affording mutual guarantees of political independence and territorial integrity to great and small states alike."

Later events have magnified the significance of this notable speech of the 8th of January. It was a striking bid for peace, which indeed was not far away and it ultimately formed the general basis of the peace terms actually drafted. But it contained nothing new. Its definition of the conditions of peace was vague; its formulation of principles followed exactly along the lines developed by President Wilson ever since he had adopted the idea of a League of Nations founded upon international justice. His summing up of the main principle underlying his whole policy was merely the echo of his speeches for the past twelve-month: "The principle of justice to all peoples and nationalities, and their right to live on equal terms of liberty and safety with one another, whether they be strong or weak." The importance of the speech does not lie in its novelty but in its timeliness. It came at a moment when the world was anxiously listening and the undeniable idealism of its content assured to President Wilson, at least temporarily, the moral leadership of mankind. Unfortunately as the event proved, it promised more than could ever be secured by any single man. The President was to pay the price for his leadership later when he encountered the full force of the reaction.

As a step toward immediate peace the speech of the Fourteen Points failed. What might have been the result had von Hertling, Chancellor of

Germany, and Czernin, in Austria, possessed full powers, it is difficult to say. But the military masters of Germany could not resist the temptation which the surrender of Russia brought before their eyes. By securing the eastern front and releasing prisoners as well as troops there, they would be able to establish a crushing superiority in the west; France would be annihilated before the American armies could count, if indeed they were ever raised. Hence the heavy terms of Brest-Litovsk and Bucharest and the preparations for the great drive of March. As Wilson said, "The tragical circumstance is that this one party in Germany is apparently willing and able to send millions of men to their death to prevent what all the world now sees to be just." Thus Germany lost her last chance to emerge from the war uncrushed.

The ruthless policy followed by Ludendorff and his associates gave the President new opportunities to appeal to the peoples of the Central Empires. He incorporated in his speeches the phrases of the German Socialists. "Self-Determination" and "No annexations and no indemnities" were phrases that had been made in Germany before Russia imported them; and when they formed the text of presidential addresses, many Germans, despite themselves, doubtless felt a twinge of sympathy. Coupled with these appeals went the President's warnings that if they persisted in tying up their fortunes with those of their rulers, they must share the penalties. If Germany insisted upon making force alone the deciding element, then he must accept the challenge and abide the issue. "There is, therefore, but one response possible from us: Force, Force to the utmost, Force without stint or limit, the righteous and triumphant Force which shall make Right the law of the world and cast every selfish dominion down in the dust." Neither the appeals nor the warnings of Wilson had any effect apparent at the moment, and yet the seed was sown. During the victorious German drives of March, April, and May, opinion to the east of the Rhine seemed to have rallied firmly behind the Teuton Government; but with the first slight setbacks of the following month the process of crumbling began. An American economist and banker, Henry C. Emery, then prisoner in Germany, tells of the pessimism prevalent as early as June and the whispers of the approaching fall of the Kaiser. In his memoirs Ludendorff lays the failure of the German armies in August to the complete breakdown of the national spirit.

The end came with extraordinary speed. Already in September, after the defection of Bulgaria and the startling success of Foch's converging movement on Sedan, Germany knew that she was defeated. The Berlin Government turned to Wilson and on the 5th of October requested an armistice. At the same time Austria-Hungary made a similar request offering to negotiate on the basis of the Fourteen Points. Wilson's position was delicate. He knew in September that the end was near and prepared for the situation in some degree by sending Colonel House abroad to be ready to discuss armistice terms with the Allies. But the sudden character of the German collapse had intoxicated public opinion to such an extent that the political idealism which he had voiced ran the risk of becoming swamped. If Germany were indeed helpless and the Allies triumphant, there was the danger that, in the flush of victory, all the promises of a just peace would be forgotten. He must provide against such a contingency. On the other hand he must secure guarantees that Germany had indeed thrown off her militaristic cloak, as Prince Max of Baden, the new Chancellor, insisted; and also that under cover of an armistice she might not effect a withdrawal of her defeated armies, only to renew the struggle under more favorable conditions on her own borders. He was caught between the danger of German fraud and Allied exuberance.

There ensued a month of negotiations, during which the military victory of the Allies was further assured, as described in the preceding pages. The German Government was first asked by Wilson if it accepted the Fourteen Points and the similar stipulations made by the President in subsequent addresses. Replying in the affirmative, Prince Max then promised to acquiesce in armistice terms that would leave the military situation unchanged, and further agreed to order a cessation of unrestricted submarine warfare and of the wanton destruction caused by the German armies in their retreat. Finally he declared in answer to Wilson's demand, that the request for an armistice and peace came from a government "which is free from any arbitrary and irresponsible influence, and is supported by the approval of an overwhelming majority of the German people." The President then formally transmitted the correspondence to the Allies, and Colonel House entered upon discussions to establish with them the understanding that the basis of the peace negotiations would be the Wilsonian programme. He was successful; and the Fourteen Points, with reservation of the second, "Freedom of the seas," were accepted by the Allied governments. The Allies, on the other hand, secured President Wilson's approval of the principle that "compensation will be made by Germany for all damage done to the civilian population of the Allies and their property by the aggression of Germany by land, by sea, and from the air." Upon this understanding the details of the armistice were left to the military leaders. The terms as fixed reflected the military situation on the fighting front and the political situation in Germany and placed Germany entirely in the power of the victors without possibility of renewing the war. The conditions laid down were so stringent that until the last moment a refusal by the German delegates seemed imminent; but on the 11th of November, just before the expiration of the time limit allowed them, they accepted the inevitable.

It is a mistake to regard the armistice as forced upon the Allies by President Wilson. Many persons abroad, as in this country, felt, it is true, that it was wrong to permit the peaceful withdrawal of the German armies, even though the full military advantages of victory were secured by the armistice conditions; the Allies ought, they argued, to impress cn the Germans the magnitude of their defeat on the field of battle, and this could not be done so long as German soil had been free from warfare. General Pershing was strongly opposed to the granting of an armistice. The Allied chiefs knew, however, that although the continuation cf the fighting would lead to the surrender of a great German force, every day would cost the victorious armies a heavy toll of killed and wounded, and the advantage to be gained thereby was at least questionable. This fact was emphasized even by Marshal Foch. They hesitated, certainly, to accept the Fourteen Points as the basis for peace, for they feared lest the interpretation put upon them at the Peace Conference might rob them of what they believed to be the just fruits of victory. In both France and England there was, it is true, a body of liberal opinion which would not brook open repudiation of the ideals that Wilson had sponsored during the war and to which Allied ministers had themselves paid tribute. In each country there was another group demanding a "peace of annihilation," with the payment of all war costs by the defeated, but Lloyd George and Clemenceau feared at the moment to raise this issue. Both England and France were dependent upon

American assistance for the immediate future as they had been during the war. They needed American food, raw materials, and money. A break with Wilson, who for the moment was the popular hero of Europe, taken in conjunction with an economic crisis, might be the signal for domestic disturbances if not revolution.

Thus with Germany helpless and the Allies at least outwardly accepting his peace programme, Woodrow Wilson seemed to be master of the situation. And yet his power was more apparent than real. Apart from that moral influence which he exercised over the European liberals and which among some of the working classes was so extreme that candles were burnt before his picture, but which also was inevitably unstable and evanescent, Wilson's power rested upon the fact that he was President of the United States. But the nation was no longer united behind him or his policy, if indeed it had ever been so. That hatred and distrust which had marked the electoral campaign of 1916, and which, stifled for the moment by entrance into the war, had flamed out early in 1918 in the attack upon his war administration, now in the autumn threatened an explosion of popular disapprobation in some parts of the country. Men had long whispered "autocrat" but had generally been silenced during the war by the admonition not to weaken the government by factious criticism. Now they began to shout it from the house-tops. Because of his inability to grasp the importance of either tact or tactics, the President made the way of his opponents easy for them.

Shortly before the Congressional elections of November, at the moment when he felt the need of national support in order to strengthen his position with the Allies, the President was prevailed upon to issue an appeal to the electors, asking them to vote for Democratic candidates on the ground that the nation ought to have unified leadership in the coming moment of crisis, and that a Republican Congress would divide the leadership. There was nothing novel in such an appeal; in 1898, McKinley had begged for a Republican Congress on the ground that "this is no time for divided councils," the same ground as that taken by Wilson in 1918. Roosevelt in the same year (1898) had said: "Remember that whether you will or not your votes this year will be viewed by the nations of Europe from one standpoint only. . . . A refusal to sustain the President this year will, in their eyes, be read as a refusal to sustain the war

and to sustain the efforts of the peace commission."
Wilson's appeal in 1918 was merely an echo of
Roosevelt's in 1898. Yet it was a mistake in tactics. It enabled the Republicans to assert that,
whereas they had sunk partisan differences during
the war in order to secure the victory of the nation,
Wilson was now capitalizing the war and foreign
problems to win a partisan advantage. The result
of the elections was Republican success, assuring
to that party a slight majority in the Senate and
a goodly majority in the House after March 4, 1919.

The President made other tactical mistakes.
Instead of taking the Senate into his confidence
by entering upon numerous conferences with its
leaders, he stood upon the letter of the Constitution and gave the clear impression that he would
conduct the peace negotiations himself without
Senatorial assistance, leaving the Senators merely
their constitutional privilege of "advice and consent" when a treaty should be laid before them.
He would have done better to remember a remarkable passage in one of his own lectures, delivered
ten years before. Speaking of the difficulty of
bringing pressure to bear upon the Senate, he had
said that there is a "course which the President
may follow, and which one or two Presidents of

unusual political sagacity have followed, with the satisfactory results that were to have been expected. He may himself be less stiff and offish, may himself act in the true spirit of the Constitution and establish intimate relations of confidence with the Senate on his own initiative, not carrying his plans to completion and then laying them in final form before the Senate to be accepted or rejected, but keeping himself in confidential communication with the leaders of the Senate while his plans are in course, when their advice will be of service to him and his information of the greatest service to them, in order that there may be veritable counsel and a real accommodation of views, instead of a final challenge and contest." Had Wilson in 1918, and after, followed his own advice, the outcome might have been different. But nothing describes so perfectly the exact opposite of his attitude as the passage quoted above.

The President might at least have assuaged the sense of injury that rankled in the hearts of the Senators by asking for their advice in the appointment of the Peace Commission. Instead he kept his own counsel. He decided to go to Paris himself as head of the Commission, and chose for his associates men who were not qualified to win for him the support that he needed in the Senate or in the country. Robert Lansing, as Secretary of State, was a necessary appointment. Colonel House was probably the best-fitted man in America for the approaching negotiations, alike by his temperament, by the breadth of his knowledge of foreign questions, and by his intimacy with foreign statesmen. But at least two places on the Commission should have been given to eminent Republicans and to men universally known and respected. If Wilson was unwilling to select members of the Senate, he might have heeded public opinion which called definitely for William Howard Taft and Elihu Root. Both were pledged to the most important item of Wilson's programme, the League of Nations; both exercised wide influence in the country and in the Republican party. The Senate, with a Republican majority, would almost certainly ratify any treaty which they had signed. But the President, for reasons of a purely negative character, passed them over and with what looked to the public like mere carelessness, chose General Tasker Howard Bliss and Henry White, formerly Ambassador to Rome and Paris under Presidents Roosevelt and Taft. Both were men of ability and experience, but neither enjoyed the particular confidence of the American people; and what Americans chiefly wanted was the assurance of persons they knew and trusted, that the peace was right. In the existing state of public opinion, the assurance of the President was not in itself sufficient.

President Wilson's decision to go to Paris as a member of the Commission aroused still fiercer opposition, but had reasons infinitely more cogent. He knew that there would be great difficulty in translating his ideals into fact at the Peace Conference. He believed that he could count upon the support of liberal opinion in Europe, but realized that the leading politicians had not yet been won sincerely to his policy. The pledge they had given to accept the Fourteen Points might mean much or little; everything depended upon interpretation. A peace of justice and a League of Nations still hung in the balance. At this moment, with Germany clearly helpless, opinion abroad appeared to be tending, naturally enough, toward the old-style division of the spoils among the victors. More than one influential French and British newspaper began to sound the cry *Væ victis*. Moreover, in America broke forth a chorus of encouragement to the Allies to pay no attention to Wilsonian idealism.

On the 27th of November, shortly before the Commission sailed, Roosevelt wrote: "Our Allies and our enemies and Mr. Wilson himself should all understand that Mr. Wilson has no authority whatever to speak for the American people at this time. His leadership has just been emphatically repudiated by them. . . . Mr. Wilson and his Fourteen Points and his four supplementary points and his five complementary points and all his utterances every which way have ceased to have any shadow of right to be accepted as expressive of the will of the American people. . . . Let them [the Allies] impose their common will on the nations responsible for the hideous disaster which has almost wrecked mankind." It was frank encouragement to the Allies, coming from the American who, with Wilson, was best-known abroad, to divide the spoils and to disregard all promises to introduce a new international order, and it must have brought joy to Clemenceau and Sonnino.

Wilson feared that having won the war the United States might lose the peace: not by softness towards Germany — as yet there was no danger of that — but by forgetting the ideals for which it had entered the war, by forgetting that a peace of injustice sows the seeds of the next war, and by a relapse into the old bankrupt system of the Balance of Power. He realized that the peoples of France, England, and Italy had felt the pinch of war as the American people had never done, and that it was demanding too much of human nature to expect that their attitude would be one of moderation. He knew that in the negotiations Clemenceau and Sonnino would be definitely opposed to his programme and that he could not count upon Lloyd George. He decided therefore that he must himself go to Paris to fight for his ideals. The decision was one of tremendous significance. At the moment when domestic problems of reconstruction would be most acute, an American President was going to leave the country because of the interest of America in European affairs. The United States was now so much a part of the world system that domestic issues seemed of less importance than the danger that Europe might fall back into the old international system which had proved unable to keep the peace. The President's voyage to France was the clearest manifestation yet vouchsafed of the settled position of the United States as a world power.

If the justice of his policy and the necessity of full participation in the peace as in the war be admitted, Wilson was probably right in going to

Paris. No one else could have secured so much of his programme. No one else was possessed of the political power or the personal prestige which belonged to him. The history of the Conference was to show that when he absented himself in February and after he left Paris in June, his subordinates found great difficulty in meeting Allied opposition. But the decision of the President to attend the Peace Conference furnished fresh material for criticism at home. It was a new thing in our history; people did not understand the importance of the issues involved and attributed his voyage to vanity. Unquestionably it weakened Wilson in America as much as it strengthened him abroad. When on the 4th of December, the presidential ship, *George Washington*, sailed out of New York harbor, saluted by the wild shrieks of a thousand sirens and the showers of glittering white papers streaming from the windows of the skyscrapers, preceded by the battleship *Pennsylvania*, flanked by destroyers, with acrobatic airplanes and a stately dirigible overhead, external enthusiasm was apparently at its height. But Wilson left behind him glowing embers of intense opposition which, during the next six months, were to be fanned into a dangerous flame.

CHAPTER X

WAYS OF THE PEACE CONFERENCE

On Friday, December 13, 1918, the *George Washington* steamed slowly into Brest harbor through a long double line of gray battleships and destroyers, greeted by the thunder of presidential salutes and the blare of marine bands. Europe thrilled with emotion, which was half curiosity and half genuine enthusiasm: it was to see and applaud the man who during the past eighteen months had crystallized in speech the undefined thought of the Allied world, who represented (at least in European eyes) the strength and idealism of America, and who stood, for the moment, as the political Messiah to liberals in every country of the Old World, victors or defeated. The intensity of the curiosity as well as the sincerity of the enthusiasm was attested on the following day, when President Wilson drove through the streets of Paris, welcomed by the vociferous plaudits of the close-packed crowd. It was for him a public triumph, no greater than that accorded to King Albert of Belgium and certainly less demonstrative than the jubilations of armistice night, but nevertheless undeniably sweet to the President, who looked to popular opinion as the bulwark upon which he must rely during the difficult days ahead.

Further triumphs awaited him in his trips to England and to Italy. In London and Rome, as in Paris, he was the object of demonstrations which at times became almost delirious; more than once his admirers must have been reminded of the Biblical phrase that alludes to the honor of a prophet outside his own country. The emotion of Europe is not difficult to understand. The man in the street was ready to shout, for the war was finished and the miseries of the peace that was no peace were not yet realized. Wilson stood for Justice above everything, and the people of each country believed whole-heartedly that their particular demands were just; the President, therefore, must stand with them. To Frenchmen it was obvious that he must approve the "simple justice" of the claim that Germany pay the entire cost of the war; Italians were convinced that he would sanction their "just" demand for the annexation of Fiume.

So long as Justice remained something abstract his popularity remained secure. Could he retain it when concrete issues arose? As early as the beginning of January ebullitions of approval became less frequent. Discordant voices were audible suggesting that Wilson was too prone to sacrifice the material necessities of the war-burdened nations to his idealistic notions. People asked why he failed to visit Belgium and the devastated regions of France, so as to see for himself what sufferings had been endured. And the historian may well inquire if it were because he had not gauged the depth of feeling aroused by German war practices, or because he had determined to show the Germans that he would not let his judgment be clouded by emotion. Whatever the explanation, his popularity suffered.

Without question the original strength of President Wilson's position, resting in part upon the warmth of popular feeling, which is ever uncertain, was undermined by the delays that marked the opening of the Peace Conference. Such delays may have resulted in part from the purpose of the Allied leaders, who wished to permit public enthusiasm for Wilson to cool; they may also have been caused in part by the differences that developed over the incorporation of the League of Nations in the Treaty. But a prime cause of delay is to be found in the fact that a Peace Conference of this character was a new experience and the statesmen assembled were not quite sure how to conduct it. Too little thought had been given to the problem of organization, and the plans which had been drawn up by the French and Americans were apparently forgotten. The host of diplomatic attachés and technical advisers, who crowded the Quai d'Orsay and the hotels of Paris, had only a vague notion as to their duties and waited uneasily, wondering why their chiefs did not set them to work. In truth the making of peace was to be characterized by a looseness of organization, a failure to coördinate, and a waste of time and energy resulting from slipshod methods. In the deliberations of the Conference there was a curious mixture of efficiency and ineffectiveness; a wealth of information upon the topics under discussion and an inability to concentrate that information. Important decisions were made and forgotten in the welter of conferential disorganization.

No one could complain that delays were caused by the kind of gay frivolity that characterized the Vienna Congress a hundred years ago. The atmosphere of the Paris Conference was more like that of a convention of traveling salesmen. The Hotel Crillon, home of the American Commission, was gray and gaunt as the State, War, and Navy Building in Washington. Banquets were rare; state balls unheard of. The President who had separate headquarters, first in the Parc Monceau and later on the Place des États Unis, avoided the orthodox diversions of diplomacy and labored with an intensity that was destined to result in physical collapse. The very dress of the delegates mirrored their businesslike attitude: high silk hats were seldom seen; Lloyd George appeared in the plainest of bowlers and Colonel House in his simple, black felt. Experts worked far into the early morning hours in order that principals might have statistics; principals labored even on Easter Day, and were roused from their beds at four in the morning to answer telegrams. Unique departure in the history of diplomacy: this was a working Peace Conference!

Each of the different commissions had brought to Paris a staff of attachés and experts, upon whom the principal delegates were to rely in questions of fact, and who were themselves to decide points of detail in drafting the economic and political clauses of the treaties and in determining new boundaries. The expert staff of the American Commission had been carefully selected and was generally regarded as equal to that of any other power. Compared with the foreign experts, its members lacked experience in diplomatic methods, no doubt, but they were as well or better equipped with exact information. There is an instance of an American expert on a minor commission asking that a decision be altered in view of new facts just brought to light, and offering to place those facts in detail before the commission. "I suggest," said a foreign delegate, "that we accept the amendment without investigation. Hitherto the facts presented by the Americans have been irrefutable; it would be waste of time to investigate them."

Such men as Hoover, Hurley, and Gompers were at hand to give their expert opinions on questions which they had mastered during the course of the war. Norman Davis and Thomas Lamont acted as financial advisers. Baruch and McCormick brought the wealth of experience which resulted from their administration of the War Industries and War Trade Boards. The foresight of Colonel House, furthermore, had gathered together a group of men who, organized since the summer of 1917 in what had been called "The Inquiry," had been studying the conditions that would determine new political boundaries on the basis of justice and practicability. The principal delegates could not be expected to know the details that would decide the disposition of Danzig, the fate of Fiume, the division of the Banat of Temesvar. They would need some one to tell them the amount of coal produced in the Saar Basin, the location of mines in Teschen, the ethnic character of eastern Galicia, the difference between Slovaks and Ruthenians. It was all very well to come to the Conference with demands for justice, but our commissioners must have cold facts to support those demands. The fact that exact information was available, and played a rôle in the decisions of the Conference, marks a step forward in the history of diplomatic relations.

Contrary to general expectation and rumor, Wilson, although he disregarded the American Commissioners, except Colonel House, made constant use of the various experts. On the *George Washington* he had told a group of them that he would rely absolutely upon the results of their investigations. "Tell me what's right," he had said, "and I'll fight for it. Give me a guaranteed position." During the negotiations he called in the experts for daily consultations; they sat behind him at the sessions of the Council of Ten and on the sofa beside him in the Council of Four. Their advice was not always followed to the letter; in the Shantung issue it was reluctantly discarded; but in such important matters as the Fiume problem, Wilson rested his case wholly upon the knowledge and opinions of the experts.

In defiance of the example of the Congress of Vienna, which never formally gathered in plenary session, the Paris Conference met with all delegates for the first time, on January 18, 1919. It was a picturesque scene, cast in the long Clock Room of the Quai d'Orsay, the conventional black of the majority of delegates broken by the horizon-blue uniform of Marshal Foch, the natty red-trimmed khaki of British staff officers, and the white flowing robes and golden headdress of the Arabian Emir Faisal; down the center of the room ran the traditionally diplomatic green baize tables behind which sat the delegates; attachés and press correspondents crowded into the corners or peered around the curtains of adjoining rooms; at the end, in front of the white marble fireplace, sat the dominating personalities of the Allied world. But such plenary sessions were not to witness the actual work of the Conference, nor was Wilson's demand for "open covenants openly arrived at" to be translated literally into accomplishment. To conduct the Peace Conference by sessions open to the public was obviously not feasible. There were too many delegates. Time, which was precious beyond evaluation, would be lost in the making of speeches for home consumption. More time would be lost in translation of the Babel of languages. Frankness and directness of negotiation would be impossible, for if the papers should print what the delegates said about each other there would be a national crisis every day. Finally, a congress is by nature ill-adapted for the study of intricate international problems, as was later to be illustrated in the history of the United States Senate.

The representatives of the larger European Powers had assumed that the direction of the Conference would be taken by a small executive committee, corresponding to the Supreme War Council, and to this President Wilson agreed. Such a committee would necessarily meet in secret, in order that it might not be hampered by formalities and that there might be frank speech. Only a brief communiqué, stating the subject of discussion and the decision reached, would be issued to the press. The committee would provide for the executive measures that must be taken to oppose the growth of economic and political anarchy in central and southeastern Europe, would distribute the problems that were to be studied by special commissions, and would formulate or approve the solutions to those problems. It would supervise the drafting of the treaties and present them to the plenary conference in practically final form. Since the bulk of the fighting had been carried by the major powers and since they would guarantee the peace, this supreme council of the Conference was composed of two representatives of the major five, France, Great Britain, the United States, Italy, and Japan, the last-named now entering the sacred coterie of "Great Powers." Among the delegates of the smaller powers there was lively dissatisfaction at the exclusion from the inner council of such states as Belgium and Serbia, which had been invaded by the enemy and had made heavy sacrifices in the war; they complained also that the number of delegates allotted them was insufficient. Already, it was whispered, the phrases that dealt with the "rights of small nations" were being forgotten, and this peace congress was to be but a repetition of those previous diplomatic assemblies where the spoils went to the strong. But Wilson, who was regarded as the defender of the rights of the small states, agreed with Clemenceau that practical necessity demanded an executive council of restricted numbers, and felt that such a body could be trusted to see that effective justice was secured. In truth the President was almost as much impressed by the extreme nationalistic ardor of the small powers, as a source of future danger, as he was by the selfishness of the large.

The Supreme Council, during the early days of the Conference, was generally known as the Council of Ten. It met in the study of Stephane Pichon, the French Foreign Minister, which opened on to the garden of the French Foreign Office, and which, with its panelled walls, covered with gorgeous Gobelins picturing Ruben's story of Marie de' Medici, its stately brocaded chairs, and old-rose and gray Aubusson carpets, was redolent of old-time diplomacy. In the center, behind a massive desk, sat the president of the Conference, Georges Clemenceau — short, squat, round-shouldered, with heavy white eyebrows and mustache serving perfectly to conceal the expression both of eyes and of mouth. Ordinarily he rested immobile, his hands folded in the eternal gray gloves, on his face an expression of bored tolerance, the expression of a man who, after half a century in the political arena of France, had little to learn either of men or of affairs, even from a Peace Conference. Skeptical in attitude, a cold listener, obviously impermeable to mere verbiage and affected by the logic of facts alone, he had a ruthless finger ready to poke into the interstices of a loosely-woven argument. Clemenceau spoke but rarely, in low even tones, with a paucity and awkwardness of gesture surprising in a Latin; he was chary of eloquence, disdaining the obvious arts of the rhetor, but he had at his command an endless string of biting epigrams, and his satire wounded with a touch so sharp that it was scarcely felt or seen except by the unfortunate recipient. Upon infrequent occasion, in the course of hot debate, some one would pierce his armor and touch him upon the unguarded quick; then the man was transformed, the eyebrows would shoot up, the eyes flash, the mustache bristle, the voice vibrate, and the invective which he poured forth scalded like molten lead. One understood at such a moment why he was called "the Tiger." But such outbursts were rare. More characteristic of his method of debate was the low-voiced ironical phrase, when his arid humor crackled like a wireless message.

Clemenceau dwarfed the other French delegates, with a single exception, not alone by the magic of his personality but by the grip which he had on the imagination of France. The people remembered that long career, beginning with the early days of the Republic and culminating with the miracle of the political salvation he brought to France in the dark days of 1917, when the morale of the nation was near the breaking-point, and which made possible the military victory of Foch. France was grateful. He had no political party in the Chamber upon which to rely, but the nation was behind him, at least for the moment. "If I should die now," he is reported to have said during the early days of the Conference, "France would give me a great funeral. If I live six months, no one knows what may happen." For Clemenceau was a realist; he did not permit himself the luxury of being deceived even by the good qualities of his own countrymen. If he feared anything it was the domination of politics by the impractical. Mankind must be taken as it is and not as we should like it to be. He was troubled by what he called the "noble simplicity" of Wilson. Statesmen must be inspired by the sacred egotism which provides for the material safety and progress of their own nation. Above all, in his mind, France was particularly vulnerable and thus must insist upon particular means of defense against the secular enemy across the Rhine.

Behind Clemenceau, in the Council, hovered his friend and Foreign Secretary, Stephane Pichon. More in evidence, however, was André Tardieu, who alone of the French delegates remained undwarfed by the Prime Minister. Journalist, politician, captain of Blue Devils, Franco-American Commissioner, now the youngest of the French peace commission, Tardieu, more than any one else supplied the motive energy that carried the treaty to completion. Debonair and genial, excessively practical, he was the "troubleman" of the Conference: when difficulties arose over the Saar, or Fiume, or reparations, Tardieu was called in to work with a special committee and find a compromise. Not a regular member of the Council of Ten, he was nevertheless at Clemenceau's elbow, and especially after the attempt on the latter's life, he labored day and night on the details which were too much for the strength and time of the older man.

On Clemenceau's right, and half facing him, sat the two American delegates, Wilson and Lansing. The President, to the surprise of many, was by no means the awkward college professor lost among practical politicians. His speech was slow and his manner might almost be called ponderous, but the advisers who whispered over his shoulder, during the course of the debate, attested the rapidity with which his mind operates and his skill in catching the points suggested. There was far less of the dogmatic doctrinaire in his attitude than had been looked for. Occasionally his remarks bordered upon the sententious, but he never " orated," invariably using a conversational tone; many of his points were driven home by humorous allusions or anecdotes rather than by didactic logic. Like that of the other delegates his manner was informal. During the cold days of late January he walked about the room during discussions in order to keep his feet warm. Indeed the proceedings of the Council of Ten were characterized by a noted absence of stiffness. It was evidently expected that the prestige which Wilson possessed among the masses would evaporate in this inner council; but nothing of the kind was apparent. It was not uninteresting to note that when a point was raised every one looked involuntarily to see how it would be taken by the President; and when the delegates of the smaller Powers appeared before the Council they addressed their remarks almost directly at him. Lansing spoke seldom, but then with force and conviction, and was evidently more troubled than Wilson by the compromises with expediency which the Americans were compelled to make. His attention was never distracted by the sketches which he drew without ceasing, during the course of the debates—grotesque and humorous figures, much in demand by every one present as mementos of the Conference.

Next on the right sat David Lloyd George, with thick gray hair and snapping Celtic eyes. Alert and magnetic, he was on the edge of his chair, questioning and interrupting. Frankly ignorant of the details of continental geography and politics, naïve in his inquiries, he possessed the capacity for acquiring effective information at lightning speed. Unfortunately he was not over-critical and the source of his information was not invariably the highest authority; he was prone to accept the views of journalists rather than those of his own Foreign Office. Effervescent as a bottle just rid of its cork, he was also unstable, twisting and veering in his suggestions; not so much blown about by the winds of hostile criticism, to which he paid but little attention, as carried on by the shifting tides of political events at home. For his eye was always across the Channel, calculating the domestic effect of each treaty provision. Few could resist his personal magnetism in conversation and no one would deny him the title of master-politician of his age. During the first weeks of the Conference, Wilson seems to have fallen under the spell of Lloyd George to some extent, who showed himself quite as liberal as the President in many instances. But Wilson was clearly troubled by the Welshman's mercurial policy, and before he finally left for America, found relief in the solid consistency of Clemenceau. He always knew where the French Premier stood, no matter how much he might differ from him in point of view.

Beside Lloyd George, a perfect foil, sat Arthur J. Balfour, assuming the attitude habitual to him after long years in the House of Commons — head on the back of his chair, body reclining at a comfortable angle, long legs stretched in front, hands grasping the lapels of his coat, eyes at frequent intervals closed. Rising, he overtopped every one present, white and bent though he was, in physical stature as he did also in pure intellectual power. Graceful in tone and expression his outlook was the philosophical, possibly over-tolerant for the exigencies of the situation, although upon occasion his judgment proved a valuable counterweight to the hasty enthusiasm of Lloyd George. But Balfour, like Lansing, was sometimes treated with scant consideration by his chief and by no means exercised the influence which his experience and capacity would lead one to expect.

On the right of the British delegates sat the two Japanese, silent, observant, their features immobile as the Sphinx. It was a bold man who would attempt to guess the thoughts masked by their impassive faces. They waited for the strategic moment when they were to present their special claims; until then they attended all meetings, scarcely speaking a word, unwilling to commit themselves. Upon one occasion, in a minor commission, the Japanese delegate held the deciding vote, the other four delegations being tied; when asked by the chairman how he voted, whether with the French and Americans or with the British and Italians, the Japanese responded simply, "Yes." Next the Japanese, but facing Clemenceau and about twelve feet from him, were the Italians:

Sonnino with his close-cropped white bullet head and heavy drooping mustache, his great Roman nose coming down to meet an equally strong out-jutting chin, his jaw set like a steel latch. The hawklike appearance of the man was softened in debate by the urbanity of his manner and the modulations of his voice. Orlando was less distinctive in appearance and character. Eloquent and warm-hearted, he was troubled by the consciousness that failure to secure the full extent of Italian claims spelled the downfall of his ministry in Rome. It is of some historical importance that Sonnino, who spoke perfect English with just a trace of Etonian inflection, was the more obstinate in his demands; Orlando, who showed himself inclined to compromise, spoke no English and therefore could come into intellectual contact with Wilson and Lloyd George only through the medium of an interpreter.

Proceedings were necessarily in both French and English, because none of the big men except Clemenceau and Sonnino used the two languages with comfort. The interpreter, Mantoux, who sat behind Clemenceau, was no mere translator. A few notes scribbled on a pad were sufficient for him to render the sense of a speech with keen accuracy and frequently with a fire and a pungency that surpassed the original. He spoke always in the first person as though the points made in debate were his own, and the carrying of each particular point the ideal nearest his heart. Behind the principals, the "Olympians," as they came to be called, were the experts and attachés, with long rolls of maps and complex tables of statistics, ready to answer questions of detailed facts. In truth there was more reference to sources of exact information by the chief delegates than would have been expected by the student of former diplomatic practices.

In the center of the room, facing the Olympians, stood or sat the particular claimant or expert witness of the séance. Now it might be Marshal Foch, with wrinkled, weary, war-worn visage, and thin rumpled hair, in shabby uniform, telling of Germany's failure to fulfill the armistice conditions; one would meet him later in the corridor outside — like Grant, he was apt to have the stump of a black cigar in the corner of his mouth — usually shaking his head ominously over the failure of the politicians to treat Germany with the requisite severity. Or the claimant before the Ten might be the grave, self-contained Venizelos, once outlaw and revolutionary, now, after many turns of fortune's wheel,

master of Greece and perhaps the greatest statesman of them all. Then again would appear the
boyish Foreign Minister of the Czecho-Slovak
Republic, Edward Benes, winning friends on all
sides by his frank sincerity and ready smile; or,
perfect contrast, the blackbearded Bratiano of
Rumania, claiming the enforcement of the secret
treaty that was to double the area of his state.
Later, Paderewski came from Warsaw, his art
sacrificed on the altar of patriotism, leonine in
appearance, but surprisingly untemperamental in
diplomatic negotiation.

To each of these and to many others who presented problems for immediate settlement the
Council listened, for it had not merely to draw up
treaties and provide for the future peace of the
world, but also to meet crises of the moment. The
starving populations of central and southeastern
Europe must be fed; tiny wars that had sprung up
between smaller nationalities must be attended to
and armistice commissions dispatched; the reha-
bilitation of railroads and river transportation demanded attention; coal mines must be operated and
labor difficulties adjusted. This economic renais-
sance had to be accomplished in face of nationalistic quarrels and the social unrest that threatened

to spread the poison of communistic revolution as far west as the Rhine and the Adriatic.

From the beginning it was clear that the actual drafting of the treaty clauses would have to be undertaken by special commissions. The work could never be completed except by a subdivision of labor and the assignment of particular problems to especially competent groups. As the Council of Ten faced the situation, they decided that the number of the commissions must be increased. By the beginning of February the work was largely subdivided. There was a commission headed by President Wilson working on the League of Nations, while others studied such problems as responsibility for the war, reparations, international labor legislation, international control of ports, waterways, and railways, financial and economic problems, military, naval, and aerial questions. When the Council of Ten found themselves puzzled by the conflicting territorial claims of different Allied nations, they decided to create also special territorial commissions to study boundaries and to report their recommendations back to the Supreme Council. It was President Wilson, chafing at the early delays of the Conference, who eagerly adopted a suggestion of Colonel House to the effect that time might be saved if the experts of the different states attacked boundary problems and thus relieved the strain upon the time and nerves of the Olympians, who could not be expected to know or understand the details of each question. The suggestion was approved by the chiefs of the Allied governments. There were five such territorial commissions, which were in turn subdivided, while a single central territorial commission was appointed to coördinate the reports.

The more important commissions, such as that upon the League of Nations, were composed of plenipotentiaries and included generally representatives from the smaller states. The reparations, financial, and labor commissions were made up of business men and financiers, the American representatives including such figures as Lamont, Norman Davis, Baruch, and McCormick. The territorial commissions were composed of the representatives of the four principal Powers; most of the European delegates, who were in some cases also plenipotentiaries, were chosen from the staffs of the Foreign Offices, and included such men as Sir Eyre Crowe, Jules Cambon, Tardieu, and Salvago Raggi. The American delegates were generally members of the Inquiry, men who had been

working on these very problems for more than a
year. The special commissions worked with care
and assiduity, and their decisions rested generally on facts established after long discussion. To
this extent, at least, the Paris Conference was
characterized by a new spirit in diplomacy.

Upon the reports of these commissions were
based the draft articles of the treaties, which were
then referred back to the Supreme Council. By
the time the reports were finished, that body had
divided into two smaller bodies: the Council of
Foreign Ministers, and the Council of Premiers,
composed of Clemenceau, Lloyd George, Wilson,
and Orlando. The latter body, which came to be
known as the Council of Four, or, colloquially,
the "Big Four," naturally assumed complete direction. It was unfortunate certainly that a congress which had started with the cry of "open
covenants" should thus find itself practically
resolved into a committee of four. Disappointed liberals have assumed that the inner council
was formed with the object of separating President Wilson from contact with popular ideas
and bringing him to acceptance of the old-style
peace desired by Clemenceau. In reality the Council of Four was simply a revival of the informal

committee which had sat during the autumn of 1918, when Colonel House, Lloyd George, and Clemenceau had met by themselves to formulate the policy to be adopted when Germany presented her demand for an armistice. When Wilson left Paris in February, Colonel House, who became chiefly responsible for the American side of nego- tiations, found the Council of Ten unwieldy. It was attended by as many as thirty or forty per- sons, some of whom seemed inclined to spread col- ored accounts of what was going on, and the very size of the meeting tended toward the making of speeches and the slowing-down of progress. Furthermore, at that time Clemenceau, confined to his house by the wound inflicted by a would-be assassin, was unable to attend the sessions of the Council of Ten. It was natural, therefore, that the three statesmen who had worked so effectively the preceding autumn should now renew their private conferences. When Wilson returned to Paris in March, and learned from Colonel House how much more rapidly the small committee was able to dis- pose of vexatious questions, he readily agreed to it. Nor is there any valid evidence extant to show that his influence was seriously impaired by the change, although the sessions of the Council of Four took on a greater appearance of secrecy than had been desired by Colonel House.

The Council of Four acted as a board of review and direction rather than of dictators. When the reports of the expert commissions were unanimous they were generally accepted with little or no alteration. When a divided report was sent up, the Four were compelled to reach a compromise, since every delay threatened to give new opportunity to the forces of social disorder in Germany and southeastern Europe. The Council met ordinarily in the house used by President Wilson, on the Place des États-Unis. Some of the conferences were held in a small room downstairs without the presence of secretaries or advisers; frequently, however, the experts were called in to meet with the chiefs in the large front room upstairs, and would often monopolize the discussion, the Four playing the part of listeners merely. Formality was dispensed with. During a debate upon the southern boundary of Austria, President Wilson might have been seen on all fours, kneeling on the floor and tracing out the suggested frontier on a huge map, while other peace commissioners and experts surrounded him, also on their hands and knees. Hours of labor were long. There was, certainly, much discussion that hinged upon selfish nationalist interests, but also much that was inspired by a sincere desire to secure the solution that would permanently restore the tranquillity of Europe.

The presence of President Wilson did much to maintain the idealism that jostled national self-seeking in the final drafting of the treaties. Though he lacked the political brilliance of Lloyd George and had not the suppressed but irresistible vehemence that characterized Clemenceau, his very simplicity of argument availed much. He was not destined to carry through the full programme of idealism as set out in the Fourteen Points, at least not as interpreted by most liberals. He could not secure the peace of reconciliation which he had planned, but even with his popularity in France, Belgium, and Italy lost, and his prestige dimmed, he retained such a strong position in the Council of Four that he was able to block some of the more extreme propositions advanced by imperialist elements, and, more positively, to secure what he had most at heart, the League of Nations. Whether he yielded more than he gained is a question which demands more detailed consideration.

CHAPTER XI

BALANCE OF POWER OR LEAGUE OF NATIONS?

WHATEVER mistakes President Wilson made at Paris, he did not greatly underestimate the difficulties of his task when he set forth from the United States. The liberal utterances of the Allied chiefs during the war had never succeeded in winning his sincere confidence; more than once he had even intimated that he did not consider their governments completely representative of public opinion. He anticipated a struggle with Clemenceau and Lloyd George over the amount of indemnity which was to be demanded from Germany, as well as over the territory of which she was to be deprived. Their formal approval of the Fourteen Points had been a cause of intense satisfaction to him, but he realized definitely that they would make every effort to interpret them in terms of purely national self-interest. This he regarded as the greatest difficulty to be met at Paris. The second difficulty lay in the extreme demands that were being made by the smaller nationalities, now liberated from Teuton dominion or overlordship. Poland, Rumania, Serbia, Greece, were all asking for territory which could only be assigned to them on the ancient principle of the division of spoils among the victors. The spirit of nationalism which had played a rôle of so much importance in the antecedents of the war, as well as in the downfall of the Central Empires, now threatened to ruin the peace. As we have seen, it was partly because of this second danger that Wilson agreed to the exclusion of the smaller states from the Supreme Council of the Allies.

Upon the details of the treaties, whether of an economic or a territorial character, the President did not at first lay great stress. He was interested chiefly in the spirit that lay behind the treaties. The peace, he insisted, must be one of justice and, if possible, one of reconciliation. More concretely, the great point of importance was the establishment of a League of Nations; for the President believed that only through the building up of a new international system, based upon the concert of all democratic states, could permanent justice and amity be secured. Only a new system could suffice to prevent the injustice that great states work upon small, and to stamp out the germs of future war. It would be the single specific factor that would make this treaty different from and better than treaties of the past. The ultimate origin of the great war was less to be sought in the aspirations and malevolence of Germany, he believed, than in the disorganized international system of Europe. Unless that were radically reformed, unless a régime of diplomatic coöperation were substituted for the Balance of Power, neither justice nor peace could last. The old system had failed too often.

Wilson does not seem to have formulated definitely before he reached Paris the kind of League which he desired to see created. He was opposed to such intricate machinery as that proposed by the League to Enforce Peace, and favored an extremely simple organization which might evolve naturally to meet conditions of the future. The chief organ of a League, he felt, should be an executive council, possibly composed of the ambassadors to some small neutral power. If trouble threatened in any quarter, the council was to interfere at once and propose a settlement. If this proved unsuccessful, a commercial boycott might be instituted against the offending state: it was to be outlawed, and, as

Wilson said, "outlaws are not popular now." He regarded it as important that the German colonies should not be divided among the Allies, but should be given to the League, to be administered possibly through some smaller power; for an institution, he felt, is always stabilized by the possession of property.

Such were, broadly speaking, the ideas which seemed uppermost in the President's mind when he landed in France, and which he was determined should form the basis of the peace. He anticipated opposition, and he was in a measure prepared to fight for his ideals. But he failed adequately to appreciate the confusion which had fallen upon Europe, after four years and more of war, and which made the need of a speedy settlement so imperative. If he had gauged more accurately the difficulties of his task he would have been more insistent upon the drafting of a quick preliminary peace, embodying merely general articles, and leaving all the details of the settlement to be worked out by experts at their leisure. He might thus have utilized his popularity and influence when it was at its height, and have avoided the loss of prestige which inevitably followed upon the discussion of specific issues, when he was compelled to take a stand opposed to the national aspirations of the various states. Such a general preliminary treaty would have gone far towards restoring a basis for the resumption of normal political and economic activity; it would have permitted Wilson to return to the United States as the unquestioned leader of the world; it would have blunted the edge of senatorial opposition; and finally it might have enabled him to avoid the controversies with Allied leaders which compelled him to surrender much of his original programme in a series of compromises.

It is only fair to Wilson to remember that his original plan, in November, was to secure such a preliminary treaty, which was to embody merely the general lines of a territorial settlement and the disarmament of the enemy. The delays which postponed the treaty were not entirely his fault. Arriving in France on the 13th of December, he expected that the Conference would convene on the seventeenth, the date originally set. But days passed and neither the French nor the British took steps toward the opening of negotiations. They had not even appointed their delegates. Lloyd George sent messages of welcome from across the Channel, but explained that domestic affairs detained him in England. Conscious of the struggle that was likely to arise between the "practical" aspirations of Europe and the "idealism" of America, the Allied leaders evidently were in no hurry to give to the exponent of the ideal the advantage of the popular support that he enjoyed during the early days following his arrival upon European shores. Hence it was not until the second week of January that the delegations began to assemble at Paris. In the interval Wilson had become involved in various detailed problems and he had lost the opportunity, if indeed it ever offered, to demand immediate agreement on preliminary terms of peace.

Notwithstanding the delays, the President secured an early triumph in the matter which he had closest at heart, namely, a League of Nations and its incorporation in the Treaty. Clemenceau had taken issue publicly with Wilson. When the President, in the course of his English speeches, affirmed that this was the first necessity of a world which had seen the system of alliances fail too often, the French Premier replied in the Chamber of Deputies, on the 29th of December, that for his part he held to the old principle of alliances which had saved France in the past and must save her in the future, and that his sense of the practical would not

be affected by the *"noble candeur"* of President
Wilson. The polite sneer that underlay the latter
phrase aroused the wrath of the more radical deputies, but the Chamber gave Clemenceau an overwhelming vote of confidence as he thus threw
down the gage. In the meantime Lloyd George had
shown himself apparently indifferent to the League
and much more interested in what were beginning
to be called the "practical issues."

With the opening of the Conference, however, it
soon became apparent that Wilson had secured the
support of the British delegates. It is possible that
a trade had been tacitly consummated. Certain it
is that the "freedom of the seas," which the British
delegates were determined should not enter into
the issues of the Peace Conference and which had
threatened to make the chief difficulty between
British and Americans, was never openly discussed.
Had Wilson decided to drop or postpone this most
indefinite of his Fourteen Points, on the understanding that the British would give their support
to the League? At all events, the League of Nations
was given an important place on the programme
of deliberations, and at the second of the plenary
sessions of the Conference, held on January 25, 1919,
the principle of a League was approved without a

dissentient voice; it was also decided that the League should be made an integral part of the Treaty. Wilson, in addition to acquiring British support had won that of the Italians, to whom he had promised his aid in securing the Brenner frontier in the Tyrol. Clemenceau, according to an American delegate, "had climbed on the band-wagon."

The President's victory was emphasized when he also won the Europeans and the representatives of the British overseas Dominions to acceptance of the principle of "mandatories," according to which the German colonies were not to be distributed as spoils amongst the victors, but to become the property of the League and to be adminstered by the mandatory states, not for their own benefit but for that of the colonies. The victory was not complete, since Wilson's first intention had been that the mandatory states should not be the great powers, but such states as Holland or one of the Scandinavian nations. He was compelled to admit the right of the British and French to take over the colonies as mandatories. Even so, the struggle over the issue was intense, Premier Hughes of Australia leading the demand that the German colonies should be given outright to the Allies and the British self-governing Dominions. Again the support of Lloyd George brought success to the American policy.

In order to assure his victory in the foundation of a League of Nations, it was necessary that before returning home Wilson should see some definite scheme elaborated. Until the 14th of February he labored with the special committee appointed to draft a specific plan, which included much of the best political talent of the world: Lord Robert Cecil, General Smuts, Venizelos, Léon Bourgeois. In order to avoid the criticism that consideration of a League was delaying the preparation of peace terms, the commission met in the evenings so as not to interrupt the regular meetings of the Council of Ten. It was a *tour de force*, this elaboration of a charter for the new international order, in less than three weeks. At times the task seemed hopeless as one deadlock after another developed. Wilson, who presided over the commission, lacked the skill and courage displayed by Clemenceau in his conduct of the plenary sessions, and proved unable to prevent fruitless discussion; possibly he feared lest he be regarded as autocratic in pushing his pet plan. At all events precious moments were dissipated in long speeches, and general principles threatened to be lost in a maze of details. With but two days left before the plenary session of the Conference and the date set for Wilson's sailing, the commission had approved only six of the twenty-seven articles of the Covenant. Fortune intervened. The presence of Wilson was demanded at the Council of Ten and his place as chairman was taken by Lord Robert Cecil. The latter showed himself effective. Ably seconded by Colonel House, he passed over all details and pushed the final stages of the report through at top speed; on the 14th of February the Covenant of the League was completed. It was sanctioned by the plenary session of the Conference that afternoon, and in the evening Wilson left for America with the document in his pocket. Doubtless it seemed to him that the major portion of his task had been accomplished.

The mechanism of the League thus proposed is said to have been largely evolved by Smuts and Cecil, but it coincided roughly with the ideas that Wilson had already conceived. Much of the language of the Covenant is Wilson's; its form was mainly determined by the British and American legal experts, C. J. B. Hurst and D. H. Miller. It provided for an executive council representing nine powers, and a deliberative assembly of all the members of the League. The Council must meet annually and take under advisement any matters threatening to disturb international peace. Its recommendations must be unanimous. The Assembly was entirely without executive power. The members of the League were to agree not to make war without first submitting the matter under dispute to arbitration or to the consideration of the Council. Failure to abide by this agreement would constitute an act of war against the League, which upon recommendation of the Council, might boycott the offending state economically or exercise military force against it. The Covenant declared it "to be the friendly right of each Member of the League to bring to the attention of the Assembly or of the Council any circumstance whatever affecting international relations which threatens to disturb international peace or the good understanding between nations upon which peace depends." The members of the League, furthermore, undertook "to respect and preserve as against external aggression the territorial integrity and existing independence of all members of the League. In case of any such aggression the Council shall advise upon the means by which this obligation shall be fulfilled" (Article

X). These two provisions embodied the particular contributions of Wilson to the Covenant, who believed that the capacity of the League to preserve justice and peace depended chiefly upon them. The Covenant also provided in some measure for military and naval disarmament by giving to the Council the right to recommend the size of the force to be maintained by each member of the League, and it attacked secret diplomacy by abrogating previous obligations inconsistent with the Covenant and by providing that every future treaty must be registered and published.

If the President expected to be hailed at home as conquering hero, he was destined to bitter disappointment. He must now pay the price for those tactical mistakes which had aroused opinion against him in the previous autumn. The elements which he had antagonized by his war-policies, by his demand for a Democratic Congress, by his failure to coöperate with the Senate in the formulation of American policy and in the appointment of the Peace Commission, and which had opposed his departure in person to Paris — all those elements now had their chance. Having won a difficult victory over reactionary forces in Europe, Wilson was now compelled to begin the struggle over again at home.

And whereas at Paris he had displayed some skill in negotiation and an attitude of conciliation even when firm in his principles, upon his return he adopted a tone which showed that he had failed to gauge the temper of the people. He probably had behind him the majority of the independent thinkers, even many who disliked him personally but who appreciated the importance and the value of the task he was trying to carry through. The mass of the people, however, understood little of what was going on at Paris. The situation abroad was complex and it had not been clarified adequately by the press. Opinion needed to be educated. It wanted to know why a League was necessary and whether its elaboration was postponing peace and the return of the doughboys. Why must the League be incorporated in the Treaty? And did the League put the United States at the mercy of European politicians and would it involve our country in a series of European wars in which we had no interest?

What followed must be counted as little less than a tragedy. The man of academic antecedents with masterly powers of exposition, who had voiced popular thought during the years of the war so admirably, now failed completely as an educator of

opinion. The President might have shown that the
League Covenant, instead of postponing peace,
was really essential to a settlement, since it was to
facilitate solutions of various territorial problems
which might otherwise hold the Conference in debate for months. He could have demonstrated
with a dramatic vigor which the facts made possible, the anarchical condition of Europe and the
need for some sort of international system of cooperation if a new cataclysm was to be avoided, and
he might have pictured the inevitable repercussive
effect of such a cataclysm upon America. He might
have shown that in order to give effect to the terms
of the Treaty, it was necessary that the League
Covenant should be included within it. He could
have emphasized the fact that the Covenant took
from Congress no constitutional powers, that the
Council of the League, on which the United States
was represented, must be unanimous before taking
action, and then could only make recommendations. But the President failed to explain the situation in terms comprehensible to the average man.
However adequate his addresses seemed to those
who understood the situation abroad, they left the
American public cold. His final speech in the
Metropolitan Opera House in New York City was

especially unfortunate, for his statement that he would bring back the Treaty and the League so intertwined that no one could separate them sounded like a threat. At the moment when he needed the most enthusiastic support to curb the opposition of the Senate, he alienated thousands and lost the chance to convince tens of thousands.

These developments did not pass unnoticed in Europe. Clemenceau and Lloyd George had yielded to Wilson during the first weeks of the Conference because they could not afford to separate their fortunes from the United States, upon whom they depended for economic support, and because an open break with Wilson would weaken their own position with liberals in France and England. But now it became apparent to them that Wilson's position at home was so unstable that they might be justified in adopting a stronger tone. Each of them could point to the tangible evidence of victorious elections and votes of confidence. President Wilson could not. The party in the Senate which, after the 4th of March, would hold the majority, expressly repudiated Wilson's policy. When the President returned to Paris, on the 14th of March, he found a different atmosphere. The League was no longer the central topic of discussion. Concrete questions were uppermost. How much should Germany pay? What territory should be taken from her? How was the Kaiser to be punished? Wilson had been given the satisfaction of securing approval for the principle of the League. Now he must permit the Conference to satisfy the practical aspirations of France, England, and Italy.

It is a tribute to the personality of Wilson that by his presence at this critical juncture, when the attitude of the Allies differed but slightly, if at all, from that of the powers at the Congress of Vienna, he was able to bring back something of the spirit of justice which had been so frequently and loudly declaimed before the armistice, and to repress at least in some degree the excessive claims which demanded satisfaction in the treaties. The plans which, during his absence, had been evolved for the separation of the Covenant from the Treaty and for its postponement, and which had received the hearty support of several French and British diplomats, were quickly dropped. Wilson was able to announce without contradiction, that the Covenant would be an integral part of the Treaty, as decided on the 25th of January. Far more difficult was the situation that resulted from French and British plans for indemnities from Germany, and from the French territorial claims on the Rhine. In each of these matters Wilson could secure nothing better than a compromise.

From the day when peace dawned upon Europe, the question that had touched Allied peoples most closely was, How much will Germany pay? It was not so much the shout of the brutal victor greedy for loot, as the involuntary cry of nations which had seen their homes and factories pulverized, their ships sunk, the flower of their youth killed and maimed, and which now faced years of crushing taxation. They had carried the load of war gallantly and they would enter the struggle for recuperation courageously. But they would not endure that the enemy, which had forced these miseries upon them, should not make good the material damage that had been done. What was the meaning of the word justice, if the innocent victors were to emerge from the war with keener sufferings and more gloomy future than the guilty defeated? Another question stirred the mind of every Frenchman. For generations the eastern frontier of France had lain open to the invasion of the Teuton hordes. The memory of Prussian brutality in 1814 had been kept alive in every school; the horrors of 1870 had been told and retold by participants and eye-witnesses; and the world had seen the German crimes of 1914. From all France the cry went up, How long? It would be the most criminal stupidity if advantage were not taken of the momentary helplessness of the inevitable enemy in order to make that vulnerable frontier secure. This was not the end. Some day the struggle would be renewed. Already, within two months of the armistice, the French General Staff were considering mobilization plans for the next war. France must be made safe while she had the chance.

These feelings had such a hold on the people that the statesmen of Europe would have been overthrown on the day they forgot them. Popular sentiment was reënforced by practical considerations less justifiable. Crushing indemnities would not merely ease the load of Allied taxation and furnish capital for rapid commercial development; they would also remove Germany as an economic competitor. French control of all territory west of the Rhine would not only assure France against the danger of another German invasion, but would also provide her capitalists with a preponderating economic advantage in regions by no means French in character. Such selfish interests the Americans strove to set aside, although they never forgot their desire to secure as complete justice for the Allies as seemed compatible with a stable and tranquil settlement.

In the matter of indemnities, or reparations as they came to be called, the experts of the various powers soon established the fact that Germany would be unable to pay the total bill of reparation, even at the most conservative reckoning. There was a long discussion as to whether or not the costs of war, aside from material damage done, that had been incurred by the Allies, should be included in the amount that Germany was to pay. It was finally determined, in accordance with the arguments of the American financial delegates who were warmly supported by President Wilson, that such war costs should be excluded. On the other hand it was agreed that pensions might properly be made part of Germany's reparation bill. The two items of damages and pensions were calculated by the American experts as amounting to a total figure of not less than $30,000,000,000 present capital sum, which Germany ought to pay.

The next step was to determine how much Germany could be made to pay. By drafting too severe terms German trade might be destroyed completely and Germany left without the economic capacity to make the money that was to pay the bill. It was obvious to careful students that the total amount which she could turn over to the Allies could not be much more than the excess of her exports over imports; and that even if payments were extended over twenty or thirty years their value for purposes of reparation would probably not much exceed twenty-five billion dollars. Lloyd George in his election pledges had promised that the complete reparations account would be settled by the enemy; neither he nor Clemenceau dared to confess that the sum which could be exacted from Germany would fall far below their early promises. The British experts, Sumner and Cunliffe, continued to encourage Lloyd George in his belief that Germany could afford to pay something in the neighborhood of a hundred billion dollars, and the French Finance Minister, Klotz, was equally optimistic. At first, accordingly, Allied demands on Germany seemed likely to be fantastic.

The Americans, on the other hand, were infinitely more conservative in their estimates of what Germany could pay. Even after certain Allied experts, including Montagu and Loucheur, affirmed the necessity of scaling down the suggested sum of reparations, the difference between the American proposals and those of the Allies was serious.[1] Political considerations, however, interposed, and preventing the settling of a definite total sum which Germany must pay. Neither Lloyd George nor Clemenceau dared to go to their constituents with the truth, namely that Germany could not possibly pay the enormous indemnities which the politicians had led the people to expect. (Lloyd George, for example, had stated the sum that Germany must pay at about $120,000,000,-000.) Both the chiefs of state asserted that they were almost certain to be turned out of office as a result, with consequent confusion in the Peace Conference, and a prolongation of the crisis. The only escape seemed to be in a postponement of the problem by not naming any definite sum which Germany must pay, but requiring her to acknowledge full liability. The disadvantages of this method were apparent to the President and

[1] At first the French and British refused to name any specific sum that might be collected from Germany, requesting the Americans to submit estimates. The latter named $5,000,000,000 as representing a sum that might be collected prior to May 1, 1921, and thereafter a capital sum as high as $25,000,000,000, always provided that the other clauses in the treaty did not too greatly drain Germany's resources. After some weeks of discussion the French experts stated that if the figures could be revised up to $40,000,000,000 they would recommend them to their chiefs. The British refused to accept a figure below $47,000,000,000.

his financial advisers, for it was clear that the economic stability of the world could not be restored until the world knew how much Germany was going to pay.

Equally difficult was the problem of the French frontier. The return of Alsace-Lorraine to France was unanimously approved. The French claimed in addition, the districts of the Saar, with their valuable coal-fields, a portion of which had been left to France after the first abdication of Napoleon but annexed to Prussia after his defeat at Waterloo; and they contended that if the German territories west of the Rhine were not to be annexed to France, they must at least be separated from Germany, which had secured a threatening military position mainly through their possession. American experts had felt inclined to grant a part of the Saar region to France as compensation for the wanton destruction of French mines at Lens and Valenciennes by the Germans; but both Wilson and Lloyd George were opposed to absolute annexation of the district which the French demanded, including, as it did, more than six hundred thousand Germans and no French. Wilson was definitely hostile to any attempt to separate from the Fatherland such purely German territory as that on the left bank of the Rhine. The Allies, as well as himself, had given assurances that they did not aim at the dismemberment of Germany, and it was on the basis of such assurances that the Germans had asked for an armistice. Wilson admitted that from the point of view of military strategy the argument of Foch was unanswerable, under the old conditions; but he insisted that the League of Nations would obviate the necessity of the strategic protection asked for.

The struggle over these issues nearly broke the back of the Conference. If Clemenceau had yielded in January when the League was demanded by Wilson, it was with the mental reservation that when the "practical" issues came up, the victory should be his. The French press were not slow to give support to their Government, and within a short time the President, so recently a popular idol, found himself anathematized as a pro-German and the sole obstacle to a speedy and satisfactory peace. The more noisy section of the British press followed suit. Liberals were silenced and American idealism was cursed as meddlesome myopia. For some days the deadlock appeared interminable and likely to become fatal. In a contest of obstinacy even Wilson could be matched by Clemenceau. The increasing bitterness of French attacks upon the

Americans began to tell upon Wilson; for the first time his physical strength seemed likely to collapse under the strain. Matters were brought to a head by a bold stroke, on the 7th of April, when Wilson ordered the *George Washington* to sail for Brest. The inference was plain: the President would leave the Conference unless the Allies abated their claims.

The week of strain was followed by one of adjustment. Fearing an open break with America, Allied leaders showed themselves anxious to find a compromise, and Wilson himself was willing to meet them part way, since he realized that without France and England his new international system could never operate. Colonel House found opportunity for his tested skill and common sense as a mediator, and he was assisted by Tardieu, who proved himself to be fertile in suggestions for a practical middle course. As in the case of all compromises, the solutions satisfied no one completely. But clearly some sort of treaty had to be framed, if the world were to resume normal life and if the spread of social revolution were to be checked. At least the compromises had the virtue of winning unanimity, without which Europe could not be saved.

The indemnity problem was settled, at least for

the moment, by postponing a final definite statement of the total amount that Germany must pay. It was decided that the sum of five billion dollars (twenty billion gold marks), in cash or kind, should be demanded from Germany as an initial payment, to be made before May 1, 1921. Certain abatements were to be permitted the Germans, since this sum was to include the expenses of the army of occupation, which were reckoned as in the neighborhood of a billion dollars; and supplies of food and raw materials, which Germany might need to purchase, could be paid for out of that sum. In the second place, Germany was required to deliver interest-bearing bonds to a further amount of ten billions; and, if the initial payment of cash fell short of five billions by reason of permitted deductions, the amount of bonds was to be so increased as to bring the total payments in cash, kind, or bonds, up to fifteen billions by May 1, 1921. If a Reparations Commission, the decisions of which Germany must agree to accept, should be satisfied that more yet could be paid, a third issue of bonds, amounting to a further ten billions might be exacted. Even this total of twenty-five billions was not to be regarded as final, if Germany's capacity to pay more were determined by the Reparations

Commission. Germany was required to acknowledge full liability, and the total sum which she might theoretically have to pay was reckoned by a British expert as between thirty-two and forty-four billions. The Reparations Commission, however, was given the power to recommend abatements as well as increased payments; upon the wisdom of its members the practical application of the treaty would obviously depend.[1]

In truth the reparations clauses of the treaty, which compelled Germany to hand over what was practically a blank check to the Allies, represented no victory for Wilson. But he had at least prevented the imposition of the crushing indemnities that had been proposed, and which must have been followed by political and economic consequences hardly short of disastrous. As for the eastern frontier of France, it was agreed that the right of property in the coal mines of the Saar district should be given outright to France, as partial but immediate compensation for the damage done at Lens and

[1] The proposal of a permanent commission for handling the whole matter of reparations was made first by an American financial adviser, John Foster Dulles. The idea was accepted by Lloyd George and Clemenceau as an efficacious method of enabling them to postpone the decision of a definite sum to be paid by Germany until the political situation in France and Great Britain should be more favorable.

elsewhere. But the district itself was to be placed under the League of Nations and a plebiscite at the end of fifteen years was to determine its final destiny. The territory on the left bank of the Rhine was left to Germany, but it was to be demilitarized entirely, a condition which also applied to a zone fifty kilometers broad to the east of the Rhine. The bridgeheads on the Rhine, as well as the German districts to the west of the river, were to be occupied for periods extending from five to fifteen years, in order to ensure the execution of the treaty by the Germans. The French press contended that Clemenceau had made over-great concessions, protesting that the League would be utterly unable to protect France against sudden attack, especially since the Covenant had not provided for a general military force. In return for these concessions by Clemenceau, Wilson gave an extraordinary *quid pro quo*. He who had declaimed vigorously against all special alliances now agreed that until the League was capable of offering to France the protection she asked, there should be a separate treaty between France, Great Britain, and the United States, according to which the two latter powers should promise to come to the defense of France in case of sudden and unprovoked attack by

Germany. The treaty did not, according to Wilson, constitute a definite alliance but merely an "undertaking," but it laid him open to the charge of serious inconsistency.

Thus was passed, by means of compromise, the most serious crisis of the Conference. In France Wilson never recovered the popularity which he then lost by his opposition to French demands. In many quarters of Great Britain and the United States, on the other hand, he was attacked by liberals for having surrendered to the forces of reaction. In the Conference, however, he had maintained his prestige, and most moderates who understood the situation felt that he had done as well as or better than could be expected. He had by no means had his way in the matter of reparations or frontiers, but he had gone far towards a vindication of his principles by avoiding a defeat under circumstances where the odds were against him. More he probably could not have obtained and no other American at that time could have secured so much. The sole alternative would have been for the American delegates to withdraw from the Conference. Such a step might have had the most disastrous consequences. It was true, or Europe believed it to be true, that the Conference represented for the moment the single rallying-point of the elements of social order on the Continent. The withdrawal of the Americans would have shattered its waning prestige, discouraged liberals in every country, and perhaps have led to its dissolution. Nearly every one in Paris was convinced that the break-up of the Conference would be the signal for widespread communistic revolt throughout central Europe. By his broad concessions President Wilson had sacrificed some of his principles, but he had held the Conference together, the supreme importance of which seemed at the time difficult to over-emphasize. Having weathered this crisis the Conference could now meet the storms that were to arise from the demands of the Italians and the Japanese.

Wilson himself was to be encouraged in the midst of those difficulties by the triumph accorded him on the 28th of April. On that day the plenary session of the Conference adopted without a word of dissent the revised Covenant of the League of Nations, including the amendment that formally recognized the validity of the Monroe Doctrine.

CHAPTER XII

THE SETTLEMENT

PRESIDENT WILSON'S success in securing approval for the League as the basis of the Peace Treaty was his greatest triumph at Paris; and it was accentuated by the acceptance of certain of the amendments that were demanded in America, while those which the French and Japanese insisted upon were discarded or postponed. In comparison with this success, he doubtless regarded his concessions in the matter of reparations and the special Franco-British-American alliance as mere details. His task, however, was by no means completed, since Italian and Japanese claims threatened to bring on crises of almost equal danger.

From the early days of the Conference there had been interested speculation in the corridors of the Quai d'Orsay as to whether the promises made to Italy by the Entente Powers in 1915, which were incorporated in the secret Treaty of London, would be carried into effect by the final peace settlement. That treaty had been conceived in the spirit of old-time diplomacy and had assigned to Italy districts which disinterested experts declared could not be hers except upon the principle of the spoils to the strong. Much of the territories promised in the Tyrol, along the Julian Alps, and on the Adriatic coast was inhabited entirely by non-Italians, whose political and economic fortunes were bound up with states other than Italy; justice and wisdom alike seemed to dictate a refusal of Italian claims. The annexation of such districts by Italy, the experts agreed, would contravene directly the right of self-determination and might lead to serious difficulties in the future. Would the President sanction the application of treaties consummated without the knowledge of the United States and in defiance of the principles upon which he had declared that peace must be made? The application of the Treaty of London, furthermore, would be at the expense, chiefly, of the Jugoslavs, that is, a small nation. The Allies, as well as Wilson, had declared that the war had been waged and that the peace must be drafted in defense of the rights of smaller nationalities. Justice for the weak as for the strong was the basis of the new international order which Wilson was striving to inaugurate.

Had the struggle been simply over the validity of the Treaty of London, Wilson's position would have been difficult enough, for the Premiers of France and Great Britain had declared that they could do nothing else but honor the pledges given in 1915. But Italian opinion had been steadily aroused by a chauvinist press campaign to demand not merely the application of the Treaty of London but the annexation of Fiume, which the treaty assigned to the Jugoslavs. To this demand both the British and French were opposed, although they permitted Wilson to assume the burden of denying Italian claims to Fiume. As time went on, Orlando and Sonnino pressed for a decision, even threatening that unless their demands were satisfied, Italy would have nothing to do with the German treaty. Finally, on the 23d of April, the crisis came to a head. On that day the President published a statement setting forth the American position, which he felt had been entirely misrepresented by a propagandist press. Emphasizing the fact that Italian claims were inconsistent with the principles upon which all the Allies had agreed, as necessary to the future tranquillity of the world, he appealed directly to the Italian people to join with the United States in the application of those principles, even at the sacrifice of what seemed their own interest.

The appeal was based upon sound facts. Its statements were approved publicly by allied experts who knew the situation, and privately by Clemenceau and Lloyd George. It had been discussed in the Council of Four and by no means took Orlando by surprise. But it gave Orlando an opportunity for carrying out his threat of retiring from the Conference. Insisting that Wilson had appealed to the Italian people over his head and that they must choose between him and the President, he set forth at once for Rome, followed by the other Italian commissioners, although the economic experts remained at Paris. Orlando was playing a difficult game. He was hailed in Rome as the defender of the sacred rights of Italy, but in Paris he lacked partners. Both the British and French agreed with Wilson that Italy ought not to have Fiume. They secretly regretted the promises of the London Treaty, although they were prepared to keep their word, and they were by no means inclined to make further concessions in order to bring Orlando and his colleagues back. After a few days of hesitation, they decided to go on with the German treaty and to warn the Italians that, if they persisted in absenting themselves from the Conference, their withdrawal would be regarded as a breach of the Treaty of London which stipulated a common peace with the enemy. They also decided that Italy could not expect to share in German reparations if her delegates were not present to sign the German treaty. Such arguments could not fail to weigh heavily with the Italian delegates, even at the moment when the Italian press and people were giving them enthusiastic encouragement to persist in their uncompromising course. On the 5th of May Orlando left Rome to resume his place in the Peace Conference.

In the meantime the Japanese had taken advantage of the embarrassment caused by the Italian withdrawal, to put forward their special claims in the Far East. During the early days of the Conference they had played a cautious game, as we have seen, attending meetings but taking no decided stand upon European matters. They had even refused to press to the limit the amendment to the League Covenant which enunciated their favorite principle of the equality of races. But now they insisted that on one point, at least, Japanese claims must be listened to; their right of inheritance to the German lease of Kiau-Chau and economic privileges in the Shantung peninsula must receive recognition. This claim had long been approved secretly by the British and French; it had even been accepted by the Chinese at the time when Japan had forced the twenty-one demands upon her. It was disapproved, however, by the American experts in Paris, and Wilson argued strongly for more generous treatment of China. His strategic position, one must admit, was not nearly so strong as in the Fiume controversy. In the latter he was supported, at least covertly, by France and England, whose treaty with Italy explicitly denied her claim to Fiume. The Japanese threat of withdrawal from the Conference, if their claims were not satisfied, carried more real danger with it than that of the Italians; if the Japanese delegates actually departed making the second of the big five to go, the risk of a complete débâcle was by no means slight. Even assuming that justice demanded as strong a stand for the Chinese as Wilson had taken for the Jugoslavs, the practical importance of the Shantung question in Europe was of much less significance. The eyes of every small nation of Europe were upon Fiume, which was regarded as the touchstone of Allied professions of justice. If the Allied leaders permitted Italy to take Fiume, the small nations would scoff at all further professions of idealism; they would take no further interest either in the Conference or its League. Whereas, on the other hand, the small nationalities of Europe knew and cared little about the justice of Chinese pleas.

Such considerations may have been in the mind of the President when he decided to yield to Japan. The decision throws interesting light upon his character; he is less the obstinate doctrinaire, more the practical politician than has sometimes been supposed. The pure idealist would have remained consistent in the crisis, refused to do an injustice in the Far East as he had refused in the settlement of the Adriatic, and would have taken the risk of breaking up the Conference and destroying all chance of the League of Nations. Instead, Wilson yielded to practical considerations of the moment. The best that he could secure was the promise of the Japanese to retire from the peninsula, a promise the fulfillment of which obviously depended upon the outcome of the struggle between liberal and conservative forces in Japan, and which accordingly remained uncertain. He was willing to do what

he admitted was an injustice, in order to assure
what seemed to him the larger and the more certain
justice that would follow the establishment of the
League of Nations.

The settlement of the Shantung problem removed the last great difficulty in completing the
treaty with Germany, and on the 7th of May the
German delegates appeared to receive it. Nearly
eight weeks of uncertainty followed, taken up with
the study of German protests, the construction of
the treaty with Austria, and finally the last crisis
that preceded the signature. The terms were dras-
tic and the German Government, in the persons of
Scheidemann, the Premier, and Brockdorff-Rant-
zau, Minister for Foreign Affairs, seemed determined that, helpless as she was, Germany should
not accept them without radical modifications.
Their protests touched chiefly upon the economic
clauses and reparations, the solution of the Saar
problem, the cession of so much German territory
to Poland, and the exclusion of Germany from the
League of Nations. Ample opportunity was given
their delegates to formulate protests, which, although they rarely introduced new facts or arguments that had not been discussed, were carefully
studied by Allied experts. Week after week passed.

In certain quarters among the Allies appeared a tendency to make decided concessions in order to win the consent of the German delegates. No one wanted to carry out an invasion of the defeated country, and there was no guarantee that a military invasion would secure acquiescence. Germany's strength was in sitting still, and she might thus indefinitely postpone the peace. Was it not the wise course, one heard whispered in Paris, to sugar the bitterness of the treaty and thus win Germany's immediate signature?

Early in June, Lloyd George, evidently under pressure from his Cabinet, declared himself for a decided "softening" of the peace terms in order to secure the acceptance of the enemy. What would Wilson do? He had been anathematized at home and abroad as pro-German and desirous of saving Germany from the consequences of her misdeeds; here was his chance. Would he join with the British in tearing up this treaty, which after four months of concentrated effort had just been completed, in order to secure the soft peace that he was supposed to advocate? His attitude in this contingency showed his ability to preserve an even balance. In the meeting of the American delegation that was called to consider the British proposal, he pronounced himself as strongly in favor of any changes that would ensure more complete justice. If the British and French would consent to a definite and moderate sum of reparations (a consent which he knew was out of the question) he would gladly agree. But he would not agree to any concessions to Germany that were not based upon justice, but merely upon the desire to secure her signature. He was not in favor of any softening which would mar the justice of the settlement as drafted. "We did not come over," he said, "simply to get any sort of peace treaty signed. We came over to do justice. I believe, even, that a hard peace is a good thing for Germany herself, in order that she may know what an unjust war means. We must not forget what our soldiers fought for, even if it means that we may have to fight again." Wilson's stand for the treaty as drafted proved decisive. Certain modifications in details were made, but the hasty and unwise enthusiasm of Lloyd George for scrapping entire sections was not approved. The Conference could hardly have survived wholesale concessions to Germany: to prolong the crisis would have been a disastrous confession of incompetence. For what confidence could have been placed in statesmen

who were so patently unable to make and keep
their minds?

Still the German Government held firm and refused to sign. Foch inspected the Allied troops on
the Rhine and Pershing renounced his trip to England, in order to be ready for the invasion that had
been ordered if the time limit elapsed without signature. Only at the last moment did the courage
of the Germans fail. A change of ministry brought
into power men who were willing to accept the inevitable humiliation. On the 20th of June, the
guns and sirens of Paris announced Germany's acceptance of the peace terms and their promise to
sign, and, surprising fact, a vast crowd gathered on
the Place de la Concorde to cheer Wilson; despite
his loss of popularity and the antagonism which he
had aroused by his opposition to national aspirations of one sort or another, he was still the man
whose name stood as symbol for peace.

Eight days later in the Hall of Mirrors at Versailles, where forty-eight years before had been
born the German Empire, the delegates of the Allied states gathered to celebrate the obsequies of
that Empire. It was no peace of reconciliation,
this treaty between the new German Republic and
the victorious Allies. The hatred and distrust

inspired by five years of war were not so soon to be liquidated. As the German delegates, awkward and rather defiant in their long black frock coats, marched to the table to affix their signatures, they were obviously, in the eyes of the Allied delegates and the hundreds of spectators, always "the enemy." The place of the Chinese at the treaty table was empty; for them it was no peace of justice that gave Shantung to the Japanese, and they would not sign. The South African delegate, General Smuts, could not sign without explaining the balance of considerations which led him to sanction an international document containing so many flaws.

It was not, indeed, the complete peace of justice which Wilson had promised and which, at times, he has since implied he believed it to be. Belgians complained that they had not been given the left bank of the Scheldt; Frenchmen were incensed because their frontier had not been protected; Italians were embittered by the refusal to approve their claims on the Adriatic; radical leaders, the world over, were frank in their expression of disappointment at the failure to inaugurate a new social order. The acquiescence in Japanese demands for Kiau-Chau was clearly dictated by expediency rather than by justice. Austria, reduced in size and bereft of material resources, was cut off from the sea and refused the possibility of joining with Germany. The nationalistic ambitions of the Rumanians, of the Jugoslavs, of the Czechoslovaks, and of the Poles were aroused to such an extent that conflicts could hardly be avoided. Hungary, deprived of the rim of subject nationalities, looked forward to the first opportunity of reclaiming her sovereignty over them. The Ruthenians complained of Polish domination. Further to the east lay the great unsettled problem of Russia.

But the most obvious flaws in the treaty are to be found in the economic clauses. It was a mistake to compel Germany to sign a blank check in the matter of reparations. Germany and the world needed to know the exact amount that was to be paid, in order that international commerce might be set upon a stable basis. The extent of control granted to the Allies over German economic life was unwise and unfair.

Complete justice certainly was not achieved by President Wilson at Paris, and it may be questioned whether all the decisions can be regarded even as expedient. The spirit of the Fourteen Points, as commonly interpreted, had not governed the minds of those who sat at the council table.

The methods adopted by the Council of Ten and the Council of Four were by no means those to which the world looked forward when it hailed the ideal expressed in the phrase, "Open covenants openly arrived at." The "freedom of the seas," if it meant the disappearance of the peculiar position held by Great Britain on the seas, was never seriously debated, and Wilson himself, in an interview given to the London *Times*, sanctioned "Britain's peculiar position as an island empire." Adequate guarantees for the reduction of armaments were certainly not taken at Paris; all that was definitely stipulated was the disarmament of the enemy, a step by no means in consonance with the President's earlier policy which aimed at universal disarmament. An "absolutely impartial adjustment of all colonial claims" was hardly carried out by granting the German colonies to the great powers, even as mandatories of the League of Nations.

Nevertheless the future historian will probably hold that the Peace Conference, with all its selfish interests and mistakes, carried into effect an amazingly large part of President Wilson's programme, when all the difficulties of his position are duly weighed. The territorial settlements, on the whole, translated into fact the demands laid down by the more special of Wilson's Fourteen Points. France, Belgium, and the other invaded countries were, of course, evacuated and their restoration promised; Alsace-Lorraine was returned to France and the wrong of 1871 thus righted; an independent Poland was recognized and given the assured access to the sea that Wilson had insisted upon; the subject nationalities of Austria-Hungary received not merely autonomy but independence. Even as regards the larger principles enunciated in the Fourteen Points, it may at least be argued that President Wilson secured more than he lost. Open diplomacy in the sense of conducting international negotiations in an open forum was not the method of the Peace Conference; and it may not be possible or even desirable. The article in the Covenant, however, which insists upon the public registration of all treaties before their validity is recognized, goes far towards a fulfillment of the President's pledge of open covenants, particularly if his original meaning is liberally interpreted. Similarly the Covenant makes provision for the reduction of armaments. If the treaty did not go far in assuring the "removal of economic barriers," at all events the Conference did much to provide for an international control of traffic which would ensure to all European countries, so far as possible, equal facilities for forwarding their goods.

Apart from the Fourteen Points Wilson had emphasized two other principles as necessary to a just and permanent peace. The first of these was that the enemy should be treated with a fairness equal to that accorded to the Allies; the second was the principle that peoples should have the right to choose the government by which they were to be ruled — the principle of self-determination. Neither of these principles received full recognition in the peace settlement. Yet their spirit was infused more completely throughout the settlement than would have been the case had not Wilson been at Paris, and to that extent the just and lasting qualities of the peace were enhanced. In the matter of German reparations the question of justice was not the point at issue; the damage committed by Germany surpassed in value anything that the Allies could exact from her. As to frontiers, the unbiased student will probably admit that full justice was done Germany when the aspirations of France for annexation of the Saar district and the provinces on the left bank of the Rhine were disappointed; it was the barest justice to France, on the other hand, that she should receive the coal mines of the former district and that the latter should be demilitarized. In the question of Danzig, and the Polish corridor to the sea, it was only fair to Poland that she receive the adequate outlet which was necessary to her economic life and which had been promised her, even if it meant the annexation of large German populations, many of which had been artificially brought in as colonists by the Berlin Government; and in setting up a free city of Danzig, the Conference broke with the practices of old style diplomacy and paid a tribute to the rights of peoples as against expediency. The same may be said of the decision to provide for plebiscites in East Prussia and in upper Silesia. On the other hand, the refusal to permit the incorporation of the new, lesser Austria within Germany was at once unjust and unwise — a concession to the most shortsighted of old-style diplomatic principles.

In the reorganization of the former Hapsburg territories, Wilsonian principles were always in the minds of the delegates, although in a few cases they were honored more in the breach than in the observance. Wilson himself surrendered to Italy extensive territories in the Tyrol south of the Brenner which, if he had followed his own professions, would have been left to Austria. A large Jugoslav population on the Julian Alps and in Istria was placed under Italian rule. The new Czechoslovak state includes millions of Germans and Magyars. The boundaries of Rumania were extended to include many non-Rumanian peoples. Bulgars were sacrificed to Greeks and to Serbs. In the settlement of each problem the balance always inclined a little in favor of the victors. But the injustices committed were far less extensive than might have been expected, and in most cases where populations were included under alien rule, the decision was based less on political considerations than on the practical factors of terrain, rivers, and railroads which must always be taken into consideration in the drawing of a frontier. Wherever the issue was clean-cut, as for example between the selfish nationalism of the Italians in their Adriatic demands and the claim to mere economic life of the Jugoslavs, the old rule which granted the spoils to the stronger power was vigorously protested.

Whatever the mistakes of the Conference, Wilson secured that which he regarded as the point of prime importance, the League of Nations. This, he believed, would remedy the flaws and eradicate the vices of the treaties. No settlement, however perfect at the moment, could possibly remain permanent, in view of the constantly changing conditions. What was necessary was an elasticity that would permit change as change became necessary. If the disposition of the Saar basin, for example, proved to be so unwise or unjust as to cause danger of violence, the League would take cognizance of the peril and provide a remedy. If the boundaries of eastern Germany gave undue advantage to the Poles, the League would find ways and means of rectifying the frontier peacefully. If Hungary or Czechoslovakia found themselves cut off from seaports, the League could hear and act upon their demands for freedom of transit or unrestricted access to fair markets. That the League was necessary for such and other purposes was recognized by many notable economic experts and statesmen besides the President. Herbert Hoover insisted upon the necessity of a League if the food problems of central Europe were to be met, and Venizelos remarked that "without a League of Nations, Europe would face the future with despair in its heart." Because he had the covenant of such an association incorporated in the German treaty, Wilson accepted all the mistakes and injustices of the treaty as minor details and could say of it, doubtless in all sincerity, "It's a good job."

Conscious of victory in the matter which he had held closest to his heart, the President embarked upon the *George Washington* on the 29th of June, the day after the signing of the treaty, and set forth for home. All that was now needed was the ratification of the treaty by the Senate.

CHAPTER XIII

THE SENATE AND THE TREATY

NEITHER President Wilson nor those who had been working with him at Paris seriously feared that, after securing the point of chief importance to him at the Conference, he would fail to win support for the League of Nations and the treaty at home. They recognized, of course, that his political opponents in the Senate would not acquiesce without a struggle. The Republicans were now in the majority, and Henry Cabot Lodge, the new chairman of the Committee on Foreign Relations, had gone far in his efforts to undermine Wilson's policy at Paris. He had encouraged the Italians in their imperialistic designs in the Adriatic and had done his best to discredit the League of Nations. Former Progressive Senators, such as Johnson and Borah, who like Lodge made personal hostility to Wilson the chief plank in their political programme, had declared vigorously their determination to prevent the

entrance of the United States into a League.   The
Senators as a whole were not well-informed upon
foreign conditions and Wilson had done nothing to
enlighten them.   He had not asked their advice in
the formulation of his policy, nor had he supplied
them with the facts that justified the position he
had taken.   Naturally their attitude was not likely
to be friendly, now that he returned to request
their consent to the treaty, and the approach of a
presidential election was bound to affect the action
of all ardent partisans.

Opposition was also to be expected in the country.   There was always the ancient prejudice
against participation in European affairs, which
had not been broken even by the events of the past
two years.   The people, even more than the Senate,
were ignorant of foreign conditions and failed to
understand the character of the obligations which
the nation would assume under the treaty and the
covenant of the League.   There was genuine fear
lest the United States should become involved in
wars and squabbles in which it had no material interest, and lest it should surrender its independence
of action to a council of foreign powers.   This
was accompanied by the belief that an irresponsible President might commit the country to an

adventurous course of action which could not be controlled by Congress. The chief opposition to the treaty and covenant, however, probably resulted from the personal dislike of Wilson. This feeling, which had always been virulent along the Atlantic coast and in the industrial centers of the Middle West, had been intensified by the President's apparent disregard of Congress. More than one man of business argued that the treaty must be bad because it was Wilson's work and the covenant worst of all, since it was his pet scheme. One heard daily in the clubs and on the golf-courses of New England and the Middle Atlantic States the remark: "I know little about the treaty, but I know Wilson, and I know he must be wrong."

And yet the game was probably in the President's hands, had he known how to play it. Divided as it was on the question of personal devotion to Wilson, the country was a unit in its desire for immediate peace and normal conditions. Admitting the imperfections of the treaty, it was probably the best that could be secured in view of the conflicting interests of the thirty-one signatory powers, and at least it would bring peace at once. To cast it aside meant long delays and prolongation of the economic crisis. The covenant of the League

might not be entirely satisfactory, but something
must be done to prevent war in the future; and if
this League proved unsatisfactory, it could be
amended after trial. Even the opposing Senators
did not believe that they could defeat the treaty
outright. They were warned by Republican financiers, who understood international economic conditions, that the safety and prosperity of the world
demanded ratification, and that the United States
could not afford to assume an attitude of isolation even if it were possible. Broad-minded statesmen who were able to dissociate partisan emotion
from intellectual judgment, such as ex-President
Taft, agreed that the treaty should be ratified as
promptly as possible. All that Senator Lodge and
his associates really hoped for was to incorporate
reservations which would guarantee the independence of American action and incidentally make it
impossible for the President to claim all the credit
for the peace.

Had the President proved capable of coöperating
with the moderate Republican Senators it would
probably have been possible for him to have saved
the fruits of his labor at Paris. An important group
honestly believed that the language of the covenant
was ambiguous in certain respects, particularly as

regards the extent of sovereignty sacrificed by the national government to the League, and the diminution of congressional powers. This group was anxious to insert reservations making plain the right of Congress alone to declare war, defining more exactly the right of the United States to interpret the Monroe Doctrine, and specifying what was meant by domestic questions that should be exempt from the cognizance of the League. Had Wilson at once combined with this group and agreed to the suggested reservations, he would in all probability have been able to secure the two-thirds vote necessary to ratification. The country would have been satisfied; the Republicans might have contended that they had "Americanized" the treaty; and the reservations would probably have been accepted by the co-signatories. It would have been humiliating to go back to the Allies asking special privileges, but Europe needed American assistance too much to fail to heed these demands. After all America had gained nothing in the way of territorial advantage from the war and was asking for nothing in the way of reparations.

It was at this crucial moment that Wilson's peculiar temperamental faults asserted themselves. Sorely he needed the sane advice of Colonel House, who would doubtless have found ways of placating the opposition. But that practical statesman was in London and the President lacked the capacity to arrange the compromise that House approved.

President Wilson alone either would not or could not negotiate successfully with the middle group of Republicans. He went so far as to initiate private conferences with various Senators, a step indicating his desire to avoid the appearance of the dictatorship of which he was accused; but his attitude on reservations that altered the meaning of any portion of the treaty or covenant was unyielding, and he even insisted that merely interpretative reservations should not be embodied in the text of the ratifying resolution. The President evidently hoped that the pressure of public opinion would compel the Senate to yield to the demand for immediate peace and for guarantees against future war. His appearance of rigidity, however, played into the hands of the opponents of the treaty, who dominated the Foreign Relations Committee of the Senate. Senator Lodge, chairman of the committee, adopted a stand which, to the Administration at least, did not seem to be justified by anything but a desire to discredit the work of Wilson. He had, in the previous year, warmly advocated a

League of Nations, but in the spring of 1919 he had given the impression that he would oppose any League for which Wilson stood sponsor. Thus he had raised objections to the preliminary draft of the covenant which Wilson brought from Paris in February; but when Wilson persuaded the Allies to incorporate some of the amendments then demanded by Republican Senators, he at once found new objections. He did not dare attack the League as a principle, in view of the uncertainty of public opinion on the issue; but he obviously rejoiced in the President's inability to unite the Democrats with the middle-ground Republicans, for whom Senator McCumber stood as spokesman.

On the 19th of August a conference was held at the White House, in which the President attempted to explain to the Foreign Relations Committee doubtful points and to give the reasons for various aspects of the settlement. A careful study of the stenographic report indicates that his answers to the questions of the Republican Senators were frank, and that he was endeavoring to remove the unfortunate effects of his former distant attitude. His manner, however, had in it something of the schoolmaster, and the conference was fruitless. Problems which had been studied for months by experts of all the Powers, and to the solution of which had been devoted long weeks of intelligent discussion, were now passed upon superficially by men whose ignorance of foreign questions was only too evident, and who barely concealed their determination to nullify everything approved by the President. Hence, when the report of the committee was finally presented on the 10th of September, the Republican majority demanded no less than thirty-eight amendments and four reservations. A quarter of the report was not concerned at all with the subject under discussion, but was devoted to an attack upon Wilson's autocratic methods and his treatment of the Senate. As was pointed out by Senator McCumber, the single Republican who dissented from the majority report, "not one word is said, not a single allusion made, concerning either the great purposes of the League of Nations or the methods by which these purposes are to be accomplished. Irony and sarcasm have been substituted for argument and positions taken by the press or individuals outside the Senate seem to command more attention than the treaty itself."

The President did not receive the popular support which he expected, and the burst of popular wrath which he believed would overwhelm senatorial opposition was not forthcoming. In truth public opinion was confused. America was not educated to understand the issues at stake. Wilson's purposes at Paris had not been well reported in the press, and he himself had failed to make plain the meaning of his policy. It was easy for opponents of the treaty to muddy discussion and to arouse emotion where reason was desirable. The wildest statements were made as to the effect of the covenant, such as that entrance into the League would at once involve the United States in war, and that Wilson was sacrificing the interests of America to the selfish desires of European states. The same men who, a year before, had complained that Wilson was opposing England and France, now insisted that he had sold the United States to those nations. They invented the catchword of "one hundred per cent Americanism," the test of which was to be opposition to the treaty. They found strange coadjutors. The German-Americans, suppressed during the war, now dared to emerge, hoping to save the Fatherland from the effects of defeat by preventing the ratification of the treaty; the politically active Irish found opportunity to fulminate against British imperialism and "tyranny" which they declared had been sanctioned by the treaty; impractical liberals, who were disappointed because Wilson had not inaugurated the social millennium, joined hands with out-and-out reactionaries. But the most discouraging aspect of the situation was that so many persons permitted their judgment to be clouded by their dislike of the President's personality. However much they might disapprove the tactics of Senator Lodge they could not but sympathize to some extent with the Senate's desire to maintain its independence, which they believed had been assailed by Wilson. Discussions which began with the merits of the League of Nations almost invariably culminated with vitriolic attacks upon the character of Woodrow Wilson.

In the hope of arousing the country to a clear demand for immediate peace based upon the Paris settlement, Wilson decided to carry out the plan formulated some weeks previous and deliver a series of speeches from the Middle West to the Pacific coast. He set forth on the 3d of September and made more than thirty speeches. He was closely followed by some of his fiercest opponents. Senators Johnson and Borah, members of the Foreign Relations Committee, who might have been expected to remain in Washington to assist in the consideration of the treaty by the Senate, followed in Wilson's wake, attempting to counteract the effect of his addresses, and incidentally distorting many of the treaty's provisions, which it is charitable to assume they did not comprehend. The impression produced by the President was varied, depending largely upon the political character of his audience. East of the Mississippi he was received with comparative coolness, but as he approached the coast enthusiasm became high, and at Seattle and Los Angeles he received notable ovations. And yet in these hours of triumph as in the previous moments of discouragement, farther east, he must have felt that the issues were not clear. The struggle was no longer one for a new international order that would ensure peace, so much as a personal conflict between Lodge and Wilson. Whether the President were applauded or anathematized, the personal note was always present.

It was evident, during the tour, that the nervous strain was telling upon Wilson. He had been worn seriously by his exertions in Paris, where he was described by a foreign plenipotentiary as the hardest worker in the Conference. The brief voyage home, which was purposely lengthened to give him better chance of recuperation, proved insufficient.

Forced to resume the struggle at the moment when he thought victory was his, repudiated where he expected to find appreciation, the tour proved to be beyond his physical and nervous strength. At Pueblo, Colorado, on the 25th of September, he broke down and returned hastily to Washington. Shortly afterwards the President's condition became so serious that his physicians forbade all political conferences, insisting upon a period of complete seclusion and rest, which was destined to continue for many months.

Thus at the moment of extreme crisis in the fortunes of the treaty its chief protagonist was removed from the scene of action and the Democratic forces fighting for ratification were deprived of effective leadership. Had there been a real leader in the Senate who could carry on the fight with vigor and finesse, the treaty might even then have been saved; but Wilson's system had permitted no understudies. There was no one to lead and no one to negotiate a compromise. From his sick-room, where his natural obstinacy seemed to be intensified by his illness, the President still refused to consider any reservations except of a purely interpretative character, and the middle-ground Republicans would not vote to ratify without "mild reservations," some of which seemed to him more than interpretative.

Senatorial forces were roughly divided into four groups. There were the "bitter-enders," typified by Johnson, Borah, and Brandegee, who frankly wanted to defeat the treaty and the League outright; there were the "reservationists," most of whom, like Lodge, wanted the same but did not dare say so openly; there were the "mild reservationists," most of whom were Republicans, who sincerely desired immediate peace and asked for no important changes in the treaty; and finally there were those who desired to ratify the treaty as it stood. The last-named group, made up of Democrats, numbered from forty-one to forty-four, and obviously needed the assistance of the "mild reservationists," if they were to secure a two-thirds vote of the Senate. During October, all the amendments which the Foreign Relations Committee brought forward were defeated through the combination of the last two groups. Early in November, however, fourteen reservations were adopted, the "mild reservationists" voting with Senator Lodge, for lack of any basis of compromise with the Democrats. The effect of these reservations would, undoubtedly, have been to release the United

States from many of the obligations assumed by other members, while assuring to it the benefits of the League. The most serious of the reservations was that concerned with Article X of the covenant, which stated that the United States would assume no obligations to preserve the territorial integrity or political independence of any other country, or to interfere in controversies between nations, unless in any particular case Congress should so provide. From the moment when Wilson first developed his policy of international service, coöperative interference in order to prevent acts of aggression by a strong against a weaker power had been the chief point in his programme. It was contained in his early Pan-American policy; it ran through his speeches in the campaign of 1916; it was in the Fourteen Points. It was his specific contribution to the covenant in Paris. Article X was the one point in the covenant which Wilson would not consent to modify or, as he expressed it, see "nullified." Just because it lay nearest Wilson's heart, it was the article against which the most virulent attacks of the "die-hards" were directed.

The President denounced the reservation on Article X, as a "knife-thrust at the heart of the covenant," and its inclusion in the ratifying resolution of the Senate, spelled the defeat of ratification. On the eve of voting he wrote to Senator Hitchcock, leader of the Democratic forces in the Senate, "I assume that the Senators only desire my judgment upon the all-important question of the resolution containing the many reservations of Senator Lodge. On that I cannot hesitate, for, in my opinion, the resolution in that form does not provide for ratification but rather for nullification of the treaty. I sincerely hope that the friends and supporters of the treaty will vote against the Lodge resolution of ratification." The "mild reservationists" led by McCumber voted with the Lodge group for the resolution; but the "bitter-enders," combining with the supporters of the original treaty, outnumbered them. The vote stood thirty-nine in favor of the resolution and fifty-five against. When a motion for unconditional ratification was offered by Senator Underwood, it was defeated by a vote of fifty-three to thirty-eight.

The Republicans on the Foreign Relations Committee had succeeded far beyond the hopes of their leaders in August. They had killed the treaty, but in such an indirect fashion as to confuse the public and to fix upon the President the blame for delaying the peace. It was easy to picture the obstinacy of the President as the root of all the evil which resulted from the political and economic uncertainty overhanging our European relations. So widespread was this feeling among his natural opponents, that the Republican Senators began to assume a far loftier tone, and to laugh at the tardy efforts of the Democrats to arrange a compromise. When Senator Pomerene, after consultation with Administration leaders, proposed the appointment of a "committee of conciliation," to find a basis of ratification that would secure the necessary two-thirds vote, the motion was killed by forty-eight to forty-two. Senator Lodge announced that he would support the resolution suggested by Knox, which would end the war by congressional resolution and thus compel Wilson to negotiate a separate treaty of peace with Germany.

Intelligent public opinion, however, was anxious that the quarrels of the President and the Senate should not be allowed to delay the settlement.[1]

[1] A straw vote taken in 311 colleges and including 158,000 students and professors showed an inclination to favor Wilson rather than Lodge, but the greatest number approved compromise: four per cent favored a new treaty with Germany; eight per cent favored killing the Versailles treaty; only seventeen per cent approved the Lodge programme; thirty per cent approved ratification of the treaty without change; and thirty-eight per cent favored compromise.

Rightly or wrongly the people felt that the struggle was largely a personal one between Lodge and Wilson, and insisted that each must yield something of their contention. On the one hand, ex-President Taft and others of the more far-seeing Republicans worked anxiously for compromise, with the assistance of such men as Hoover, who perceived the necessity of a League, but who were willing to sacrifice its efficiency to some extent, if only the United States could be brought in. On the other hand, various Democrats who were less directly under Wilson's influence wanted to meet these friends of the League half-way. During December and January unofficial conferences between the senatorial groups took place and progress towards a settlement seemed likely. The Republicans agreed to soften the language of their minor reservations, and Wilson even intimated that he would consent to a mild reservation on Article X, although as he later wrote to Hitchcock, he felt strongly that any reservation or resolution stating that the "United States assumes no obligation under such and such an article unless or except, would chill our relationship with the nations with whom we expect to be associated in this great enterprise of maintaining the world's peace." It was important "not to create the impression that we are trying to escape obligations."

On the 31st of January the country was startled by the publication of a letter written by Viscount Grey, who had been appointed British Ambassador to the United States, but who had returned to England after a four months' stay, during which he had been unable to secure an interview with the sick President. In this letter he attempted to explain to the British the causes of American hesitancy to accept the League. He then went on to state that the success of the League depended upon the adherence of the United States, and while admitting the serious character of the reservations proposed by Senator Lodge, insisted that American coöperation ought not to be refused because conditions were attached. His views were unofficial, but it seemed clear that they were approved by the British Cabinet, and they received a chorus of endorsement from the French and British press.

The publication of Grey's letter opened a path to peace to both Senate and President had they been willing to follow it. The Senate, by very slight verbal softening of the language of its reservations, the President by taking the British Ambassador at his word, might have reached an agreement. The

Lodge group, however, which had shown some indications of a desire for compromise, was threatened by the "die-hards" who were determined to defeat the treaty; fearing beyond everything to break party unity, Lodge finally refused to alter the language of the strong reservation on Article X, which stated that the United States would assume no obligation to preserve the independence of other nations by military force or the use of its resources or any form of economic discrimination, unless Congress should first so provide. Inasmuch as the economic outlawry of the offending state was the means which Wilson chiefly counted upon, the reservation took all practical significance from Article X, since the delays resulting from congressional deliberation would prevent effective action. The President, possibly believing that imperialist elements abroad were not sorry to see Article X nullified, refused to accept the resolution of ratification so long as it contained this reservation. "The imperialist," he wrote, "wants no League of Nations, but if, in response to the universal cry of masses everywhere, there is to be one, he is interested to secure one suited to his own purposes, one that will permit him to continue the historic game of pawns and peoples — the juggling of provinces, the old balance of power, and the inevitable wars attendant upon these things. The reservation proposed would perpetuate the old order. Does any one really want to see the old game played again? Can any one really venture to take part in reviving the old order? The enemies of a League of Nations have by every true instinct centered their efforts against Article X, for it is undoubtedly the foundation of the whole structure. It is the bulwark, and the only bulwark of the rising democracy of the world against the forces of imperialism and reaction."

The deadlock was complete, and on March 19, 1920, when the vote on ratification was taken, the necessary two-thirds were lacking by seven votes. At the last moment a number of Democrats joined with the Republican reservationists, making fifty-seven in favor of ratification. On the other hand the bitter-end Republicans voted against it with the Democrats who stood by the President, thus throwing thirty-seven votes against ratification. It had taken the Peace Conference five months to construct the treaty with Germany in all its complexities, and secure the unanimous approval of the delegates of thirty-one states. The Senate had consumed more than eight months merely in criticizing the treaty and had finally refused to ratify it.

We are, perhaps, too close to the event to attempt any apportionment of responsibility for this failure to cap our military successes by a peace which — when all has been said — was the nearest possible approach to the ideal peace. It is clear that the blame is not entirely on one side. Historians will doubtless level the indictment of ignorance and political obliquity against the Senators who tried, either directly or indirectly, to defeat the treaty; they will find much justification for their charge, although it will be more difficult to determine the dividing line between mere incapacity to appreciate the necessities of the world, and the desire to discredit, at any cost, the work of Woodrow Wilson. On the other hand, the President cannot escape blame, although the charge will be merely that of tactical incapacity and mistaken judgment. His inability to combine with the moderate Republican Senators first gave a chance to those who wanted to defeat the treaty. His obstinate refusal to accept reservations at the end, when it was clear that the treaty could not be ratified without them, showed a regard for form, at the expense of practical benefit. Granted that the reservations altered the character of the League or the character of American participation in it, some sort of a League was essential and the sooner the United States entered the better it would be. Its success would not rest upon phrases, but upon the spirit of the nations that composed it; the building-up of a new and better international order would not be determined by this reservation or that. Wilson's claim to high rank as a statesmen would probably be more clear if he had accepted what was possible at the moment, in the hope that the League would be improved as the country and the world became better educated.

CHAPTER XIV

CONCLUSION

By the accident of history the Presidency of Woodrow Wilson, which he designed to utilize for a series of social reforms, was characterized by the supreme importance of foreign affairs. Whatever the significance of the legislative enactments of his first year of office, he will be remembered as the neutrality President, the war President, and the peace President. Each phase of his administration represents a distinct aspect of his policy and called into prominence distinct aspects of his character. It is the third, however, which gives to his administration the place of importance which it will hold in history; not merely because of the stamp which he attempted to place upon the peace, but because the two earlier phases are in truth expressive of his whole-hearted devotion to the cause of peace. The tenacity with which he held to neutrality in the face of intense provocation resulted less from his appreciation of the pacific sentiments of the nation, or a desire to assure its economic prosperity, than it did from his instinctive abhorrence of war. When finally forced into war, he based his action upon the hope of securing a new international order which would make war in the future impossible or less frequent. In his mind the war was always waged in order to ensure peace.

Whatever his mistakes or successes as neutrality President or war President, therefore, it is as peace President that he will be judged by history. Inevitably future generations will study with especial attention the unfolding of his constructive peace policy, from his declaration of the Fourteen Points to the Peace Conference. In reality his policy of international service, to be rendered by the strong nations of the world in behalf of peace and of absolute justice toward the weaker nations, was developed all through the year 1916. It was then that he seized upon a League of Nations as the essential instrument. But the true significance of this policy was hardly perceived before the speech of the Fourteen Points, in January, 1918. That speech gave to Wilson his position in the world, as preëminent exponent of the new ideals of international relations.

23

What the President demanded was nothing new. The principle of justice, as the underlying basis of intercourse between nations, has received wide support at all epochs of history; the cause of international peace, as an ultimate ideal, has always been advocated in the abstract; the idea of a League of Nations has frequently been mooted. But it was Wilson's fate to be ruler of a great nation at the moment when the need of peace, justice, and international organization was more clearly demonstrated than ever before in the world's history. Germany's cynical disregard of Belgian independence, the horrors and waste of the war for which Germany was chiefly responsible, the diplomatic disorganization of Europe, which permitted this world disaster, desired by merely a handful of firebrands— all these tragic and pitiful facts had been burned into the mind of the age. There was a definite determination that a recurrence of such catastrophes should not be permitted. The period of the war will be regarded by future historians as one of transition from the international chaos of the nineteenth century to an organization of nations, which, however loose, should crystallize the conscience of the world, preserve its peace, and translate into international politics the standards of morality which have been set up for the individual.

In this transition President Wilson played a part of the first importance. His rôle was not so much that of the executive leader as of the prophet. He was not the first to catch the significance of the transition, nor did he possess the executive qualities which would enable him to break down all obstacles and translate ideals into facts. But he alone of the notable statesmen of the world was able to express adequately the ill-defined hopes of the peoples of all nations. He gave utterance to the words which the world had been waiting for, and they carried weight because of his position. Alone of the great powers the United States had no selfish designs to hide behind fair promises of a better future. As President of the United States, Woodrow Wilson might look for the confidence of Europe; there was no European Government which could arouse similar trust. So long as the war lasted, the President's success as a prophet of the ideal was assured, alike by his ability to voice inarticulate hopes and by reason of his position as chief of the most powerful and most disinterested nation of the world.

But with the end of the war he faced a new task

and one which was infinitely more difficult. The flush of victory obliterated from the minds of many in the Allied countries the high ideals which they had nourished during the bitterness of the struggle. The moment had arrived when practical advantage might be taken from the defeat of the enemy, and it seemed madness to surrender such advantage for the sake of quixotic ideals. The statesmen of Europe once more viewed affairs through the colored prism of national selfishness. In America, where Wilsonian ideals had at best been imperfectly appreciated, men were wearied by international problems and longed for a return to the simple complexity of the business life which they understood. The President was confronted by a double problem. He must win from Europe acceptance of his programme, crystallized in the League of Nations; from his fellow countrymen he must secure the support necessary if the United States were to continue to play the rôle in world affairs which she had undertaken during the war, and which alone would make possible an effective League of Nations. To meet the difficulties of the task, President Wilson was imperfectly equipped. He lacked the dynamic qualities of a Roosevelt, which might have enabled him to carry his opponents off their feet by an overwhelming rush; he was not endowed with the tactical genius of a skillful negotiator; he was, above all, handicapped by the personal hostilities which he had aroused at home.

In Europe the President achieved at least partial success. He proved unable to marshal the forces of liberalism in such a way as to carry his complete programme to victory, and the sacrifices which he made to the spirit of selfish nationalism cost him the support and the confidence of many progressive elements, while they did not placate the hostility of the reactionaries. But he secured the League of Nations, the symbol and the instrument of the new international organization which he sought. Thereby at least a beginning was made in concrete form, which might later be developed, when the force of the post-bellum reaction had wasted itself.

At home, however, the forces of opposition proved strong enough to rob the President of what might have been a triumph. He lacked the capacity to reconcile his personal and political opponents, as well as the ability to compromise with the elements that were inclined to meet him halfway. In accordance with his basic principles he appealed from the politicians to the people. But here again he failed, whether because of personal unpopularity, or because of the poor publicity which had been given his efforts at Paris, or because of the physical breakdown which shattered his persuasive powers and finally led to his retirement from the struggle. The vindication which he sought in the presidential election of 1920 was denied him. The country was tired of a Democratic Administration and gave to the Republican candidate an overwhelming plurality. The sole comfort that Wilson could take, in the face of the election returns, was that both candidates had declared for the principle of international organization and that the most distinguished supporters of the successful Republican candidate had pledged themselves to a League of Nations.

The months that followed the President's return from Paris until the close of his administration thus form a period of personal tragedy. He had achieved a broad measure of success in Europe, where the difficulties appeared stupendous, only to have the cup dashed from his lips at the last moment in his own country. The bitterness of the experience was intensified by his physical helplessness. But we should lack perspective if we made the mistake of confusing personal tragedy with failure. His work remained uncrowned, but there was much that could never be undone. The articulate expression of the hopes of the world, which President Wilson voiced during the war, remains imperishable as a guide to this and future generations. The League of Nations, weakened by the absence of the United States but actually organized and in operation, was the President's work. Whatever the fortunes of this particular League the steps taken toward international coöperation by its foundation can never be completely retraced.

Woodrow Wilson, however, is not to be assessed by his accomplishment. It is as prophet and not as man of action that he will be regarded by history. Like the prophets of old, like Luther or Mazzini, he lacked the capacity for carrying to practical success the ideal which he preached. But to assume that he must accordingly be adjudged a failure is to ignore the significance of the ideals to which he awakened the world. Much there was that was unattainable and intangible, but its value to mankind in the development of international relations may be inestimable.

Not on the vulgar mass
Called "work" must sentence pass,

Things done, that took the eye and had the price. . . .
But all, the world's coarse thumb
And finger failed to plumb,
So passed in making up the main account;
All instincts immature,
All purposes unsure,
That weighed not as his work, yet swelled the man's
        amount.

published . . . . contains a detailed narrative of the events of each year.

BIBLIOGRAPHICAL NOTE

Thus far no adequate biography of President Wilson,
covering his career through the Peace Conference, has
been published. The most suggestive is Henry Jones
Ford's *Woodrow Wilson: The Man and His Work*
(1916) which stops with the close of the first term.
The author, a Princeton professor, is a warm personal
and political admirer of the President, but he makes
a definite attempt at critical appreciation. W. E.
Dodd's *Woodrow Wilson and His Work* (1920) is comprehensive and brings the story to the end of the Peace
Conference, but it is marred by eulogistic interpretation and anti-capitalistic bias. An interesting effort to
interpret the President to British readers in the form of
biography has been made by H. W. Harris in *President
Wilson: His Problems and His Policy* (1917). W. B.
Hale, in *The Story of a Style* (1920), attempts to analyze
the motives by which the President is inspired. But
the best material to serve this end is to be found in the
President's writings, especially *Congressional Government* (1885), *An Old Master and Other Political Essays*
(1893), *Constitutional Government in the United States*
(1908), *The New Freedom* (1913), *International Ideals*
(1919). The two last-named are collections of addresses made in explanation and advocacy of his plans
of domestic and international reform. The most

convenient edition of the President's official writings and speeches is Albert Shaw's *President Wilson's State Papers and Addresses* (1918), edited with an analytical index.

For the period of neutrality a storehouse of facts is to be found in *The New York Times Current History*, published monthly. The *American Year Book* contains a succinct narrative of the events of each year, which may be supplemented by that in the *Annual Register* which is written from the British point of view. A brief résumé of Wilson's first term is contained in F. A. Ogg's *National Progress* (1918). More detailed is the first volume of J. B. McMaster's *The United States in the World War* (1918), which is based upon the newspapers and necessarily lacks perspective, but is comprehensive and extremely useful for purposes of reference. The clearest outline of President Wilson's treatment of foreign affairs is to be found in E. E. Robinson and V. J. West's *The Foreign Policy of President Wilson, 1913–1917* (1917). The narrative is brief but interpretative and is followed by numerous excerpts from the President's speeches and state papers. The tone of the narrative is extremely favorable and President Wilson is credited with consistency rather than capacity for development, but the arrangement is excellent. More comprehensive is the edition by J. B. Scott, entitled *President Wilson's Foreign Policy: Messages, Addresses, Papers* (1918). Johann von Bernstorff's *My Three Years in America* (1920) is a well-reasoned apologia by the German Ambassador, which contains information of much value; it is not impossible for the critically minded to distinguish the true from the false. The description of

German criminal activities contained in Horst von der Goltz's *My Adventures as a German Secret Agent* (1917), should be checked up with the report of the Senate Committee of Inquiry into the German propaganda. *The Real Colonel House*, by A. D. Howden-Smith (1918), throws useful sidelights on Wilson and contains valuable material on the activities of Colonel House as negotiator before the entrance into the war of the United States.

The best general narrative of America's war effort is J. S. Bassett's *Our War with Germany* (1919); it is clear and succinct, beginning with the early effects of the war on the United States in 1914, and ending with the Peace Conference. An interesting, but irritating, account is to be found in George Creel's *The War, the World and Wilson* (1920), which is passionate in its defense of the President, and blurs truth with inaccuracy on almost every page. F. F. Kelly's *What America Did* (1919) is a brief popular account of the building of the army at home and abroad and the organization of industry: clear, inaccurate, uncritical. The most convenient summary of the organization of national resources is F. L. Paxson's "The American War Government," in *The American Historical Review*, October, 1920, which should be supplemented by the *Handbook of Economic Agencies for the War of 1917*, monograph No. 3 of the Historical Branch, War Plans Division, General Staff (1919). The former contains many references in footnotes, of which the most important are the *Report of the Chief of Staff* (1919) and the *Report of the Provost Marshal General* (1919). The published *Investigation of the War Department, Hearing before the Committee on Military Affairs* (1918) is invaluable.

The most complete information on ordnance is to be found in the report of General Benedict Crowell, *America's Munitions, 1917–1918* (1919); it is an official defense and should be read critically. A graphic picture of American accomplishments is given in L. P. Ayres's *The War with Germany; A Statistical Summary* (1919). The best account of operations in France is still General Pershing's *Report to the Secretary of War*, which is printed in *New York Times Current History*, January and February, 1920. It may be supplemented by Shipley Thomas's *The History of the A. E. F.* (1920).

The American point of view on the Peace Conference is set forth authoritatively in *What Really Happened at Paris* (1921), a collection of lectures delivered by members of the American Peace Commission and edited by Edward M. House and Charles Seymour. *Some Problems of the Peace Conference* (1920), by C. H. Haskins and R. H. Lord, is an accurate and comprehensive analysis of the territorial questions settled at Paris. The British point of view and the most important documents are given in *A History of the Peace Conference of Paris* (1920), written chiefly by British delegates and edited by H. W. V. Temperley. The French point of view is admirably presented in André Tardieu's *The Truth about the Treaty* (1921). An excellent picture of the conflict of interests and the manner in which they were decided is to be found in C. T. Thompson's *The Peace Conference Day by Day* (1920). Robert Lansing's *The Peace Negotiations* (1921) is interesting as giving the opinions of an American Commissioner who disagreed with Mr. Wilson's methods at Paris. J. M. Keynes's *The Economic Consequences of the Peace* (1920) contains an economic analysis which is more trustworthy than his brilliant, but misleading, picture of the Conference. It should not be read except in company with the authoritative and accurate *The Making of the Reparation and Economic Clauses* (1920), by B. M. Baruch. A clever but superficial criticism of President Wilson's peace policies is to be found in J. M. Beck's *The Passing of the New Freedom* (1920).

is more trustworthy than his brilliant but misleading picture of the Conference. It should not be read except in company with the authoritative and accurate *The Making of the Reparation and Economic Clauses* (1920), by B. M. Baruch. A clever but superficial criticism of President Wilson's peace policies is to be found in J. M. Keck's *The Passing of the New Freedom* (1920).

INDEX

AN OUTLINE OF THE PLAN OF THE CHRONICLES OF AMERICA

The fifty titles of the Series fall into eight topical sequences or groups, each with a dominant theme of its own—

I. *The Morning of America*

TIME: 1492-1763

THE theme of the first sequence is the struggle of nations for the possession of the New World. The mariners of four European kingdoms—Spain, Portugal, France, and England—are intent upon the discovery of a new route to Asia. They come upon the American continent which blocks the way. Spain plants colonies in the south, lured by gold. France, in pursuit of the fur trade, plants colonies in the north. Englishmen, in search of homes and of a wider freedom, occupy the Atlantic seaboard. These Englishmen come in time to need the land into which the French have penetrated by way of the St. Lawrence and the Great Lakes, and a mighty struggle between the two nations takes place in the wilderness, ending in the expulsion of the French. This sequence comprises ten volumes:

1. THE RED MAN'S CONTINENT, *by Ellsworth Huntington*
2. THE SPANISH CONQUERORS, *by Irving Berdine Richman*
3. ELIZABETHAN SEA-DOGS, *by William Wood*
4. CRUSADERS OF NEW FRANCE, *by William Bennett Munro*
5. PIONEERS OF THE OLD SOUTH, *by Mary Johnston*
6. THE FATHERS OF NEW ENGLAND, *by Charles M. Andrews*
7. DUTCH AND ENGLISH ON THE HUDSON, *by Maud Wilder Goodwin*
8. THE QUAKER COLONIES, *by Sydney G. Fisher*
9. COLONIAL FOLKWAYS, *by Charles M. Andrews*
10. THE CONQUEST OF NEW FRANCE, *by George M. Wrong*

II. *The Winning of Independence*
TIME: 1763-1815

The French peril has passed, and the great territory between the Alleghanies and the Mississippi is now open to the Englishmen on the seaboard, with no enemy to contest their right of way except the Indian. But the question arises whether these Englishmen in the New World shall submit to political dictation from the King and Parliament of England. To decide this question the War of the Revolution is fought; the Union is born: and the second war with England follows. Seven volumes:

11. THE EVE OF THE REVOLUTION, *by Carl Becker*
12. WASHINGTON AND HIS COMRADES IN ARMS, *by George M. Wrong*
13. THE FATHERS OF THE CONSTITUTION, *by Max Farrand*
14. WASHINGTON AND HIS COLLEAGUES, *by Henry Jones Ford*
15. JEFFERSON AND HIS COLLEAGUES, *by Allen Johnson*
16. JOHN MARSHALL AND THE CONSTITUTION, *by Edward S. Corwin*
17. THE FIGHT FOR A FREE SEA, *by Ralph D. Paine*

III. *The Vision of the West*
TIME: 1750-1890

The theme of the third sequence is the American frontier—the conquest of the continent from the Alleghanies to the Pacific Ocean. The story covers nearly a century and a half, from the first crossing of the Alleghanies by the backwoodsmen of Pennsylvania, Virginia, and the Carolinas (about 1750) to the heyday of the cowboy on the Great Plains in the latter part of the nineteenth century. This is the marvelous tale of the greatest migrations in history, told in nine volumes as follows:

18. PIONEERS OF THE OLD SOUTHWEST, *by Constance Lindsay Skinner*
19. THE OLD NORTHWEST, *by Frederic Austin Ogg*
20. THE REIGN OF ANDREW JACKSON, *by Frederic Austin Ogg*
21. THE PATHS OF INLAND COMMERCE, *by Archer B. Hulbert*
22. ADVENTURERS OF OREGON, *by Constance Lindsay Skinner*
23. THE SPANISH BORDERLANDS, *by Herbert E. Bolton*
24. TEXAS AND THE MEXICAN WAR, *by Nathaniel W. Stephenson*
25. THE FORTY-NINERS, *by Stewart Edward White*
26. THE PASSING OF THE FRONTIER, *by Emerson Hough*

IV. *The Storm of Secession*

TIME: 1830-1876

The curtain rises on the gathering storm of secession. The theme of the fourth sequence is the preservation of the Union, which carries with it the extermination of slavery. Six volumes as follows:

V. *The Intellectual Life*

Two volumes follow on the higher national life, telling of the nation's great teachers and interpreters:

VI. *The Epic of Commerce and Industry*

The sixth sequence is devoted to the romance of industry and business, and the dominant theme is the transformation caused by the inflow of immigrants and the development and utilization of mechanics on a great scale. The long age of muscular power has passed, and the era of mechanical power has brought with it a new kind of civilization. Eight volumes:

VII. *The Era of World Power*

The seventh sequence carries on the story of government and diplomacy and political expansion from the Reconstruction (1876) to the present day, in six volumes:

VIII. *Our Neighbors*

Now to round out the story of the continent, the Hispanic peoples on the south and the Canadians on the north are taken up where they were dropped further back in the Series, and these peoples are followed down to the present day:

The Chronicles of America is thus a great synthesis, giving a new projection and a new interpretation of American History. These narratives are works of real scholarship, for every one is written after an exhaustive examination of the sources. Many of them contain new facts; some of them —such as those by Howland, Seymour, and Hough—are founded on intimate personal knowledge. But the originality of the Series lies, not chiefly in new facts, but rather in new ideas and new combinations of old facts.

The General Editor of the Series is Dr. Allen Johnson, Chairman of the Department of History of Yale University, and the entire work has been planned, prepared, and published under the control of the Council's Committee on Publications of Yale University.

YALE UNIVERSITY PRESS
143 ELM STREET, NEW HAVEN
522 FIFTH AVENUE, NEW YORK